Illustrated Novell® NetWare® 2.x/3.x Software

Timothy K. McDonald

Wordware Publishing, Inc.

Library of Congress Cataloging-in-Publication Data

McDonald, Timothy.
    Illustrated Novell NetWare 2.x/3.x Software / by Timothy K. McDonald
        p.   cm.
    Includes index.
    ISBN 1-55622-235-1
    1. NetWare (Computer file)   I. Title.   II. Title: Illustrated
Novell NetWare two.x/three.x.
    QA76.76.O63M395   1992
    005.7'1369—dc20   91-47597
                                                              CIP

ISBN1-55622-235-1
10 9 8 7 6 5 4 3 2 1
9203

All inquiries for volume purchases of this book should be addressed to Wordware Publishing, Inc.,
at the above address. Telephone inquiries may be made by calling:

(214) 423-0090

Contents

Contents (cont.)

Contents (cont.)

Recommended Learning Sequence

Recommended Learning Sequence (cont.)

Module 1
ABOUT THIS BOOK

DESCRIPTION

This book describes the implementation and use of a Novell® network. Novell® *NetWare*® software is the best selling high-end network software on the market today and, when combined with the right hardware, can provide a very sophisticated solution to data and resource sharing. *NetWare* software is complimented by an array of add-on products, both from Novell and a number of third-party vendors, which allows the network additional capabilities. Some of the more important of these capabilities are also discussed in the book.

Today's networks can range from small workgroups consisting of a few personal computers (PCs) attached to a single fileserver to large enterprise-wide networks encompassing hundreds or even thousands of PCs sharing information with various fileservers, as well as mini and mainframe computers. Such large networks can link systems in different cities or different continents. Novell *NetWare* software provides the platform upon which to build all of these.

PC users today can choose from several widely supported operating systems. The most popular of these "desktop environments" include Microsoft DOS, MS Windows, Apple Macintosh, Unix, and OS/2. Novell *NetWare* now supports all of these. This means that the network can allow users of dissimilar applications, computers, and operating systems to work together. While this book focuses mainly on the DOS environment, it can be beneficial to all *NetWare* users.

There are numerous hardware options for use with Novell. Literally hundreds of makes and models of PCs can be used as Novell workstations, and many of them are suitable as fileservers. There are a variety of popular methods for interconnecting these computers, and a number of manufacturers of products that support each method. It is because Novell is so widely regarded as the standard for network operating systems that so many third-party vendors have chosen to make Novell-compatible hardware. The choice of *NetWare* software, in turn, continues to grow worldwide in part because of the tremendous third-party support that is available. This book covers many of the better-known options for network hardware.

Until recently there were several versions of *NetWare* being sold—each with different features and limitations. For small networks you could choose between ELS I or ELS

II. Larger networks might have used Advanced *NetWare*. Networks requiring a high degree of reliability could run *NetWare* SFT (which was available in 2 versions), and for very demanding environments there was *NetWare* 386. Fortunately, all of this has changed. *NetWare* software is now available in two basic versions—*NetWare* 2.x and *NetWare* 3.x. Though similar in many ways, they are two distinct products with different features, applications, and requirements. This book deals with both. This is important for three reasons. Some users and administrators may find themselves moving from a network that runs one version to a network running the other. Users on networks with multiple fileservers may find that both versions are present on the network. And finally, many networks that currently run *NetWare* 2.x will at some point be upgraded to *NetWare* 3.x.

The majority of this book deals with the numerous commands and utilities that are used in *NetWare* software. The use of each command is described and illustrated with examples that you can type directly at your workstation. Commonly made mistakes are pointed out and error messages are explained, relieving you of the frustration many users feel when learning a new software package. Some commands are identical in both *NetWare* software versions. Others are only available in one of the versions. Still others are found in both but are used differently. Throughout this book the distinctions are clearly made.

ORGANIZATION

The book consists of short modules which are alphabetically arranged for quick reference. There is also a *Recommended Learning Sequence* at the beginning of the book to guide you through the modules in a logical order. The learning sequence also groups the commands by type (public, system, and console) as an aid to each group of readers—installers or technicians, supervisors (network administrators), and beginning users. Like all books in the *Illustrated Series*, the modules are each divided into three main sections: The *Description* section, the *Applications* section, and the *Typical Operation* section.

There are three appendices. Appendix A is a list of Novell-related terms and definitions. Appendix B lists commands and their syntax. Appendix C is a chapter of exercises.

Turn to Module 2 to continue the learning sequence.

Module 2
AN OVERVIEW OF A NOVELL NETWORK

COMPONENTS

A Novell local area network (or LAN) consists of a hardware and software combination which allows the sharing of information and resources. While the size, layout, and applications of the Novell LAN vary widely, the basic components are as follows:

- Network Operating System
- Network Interface Cards
- One or more Fileservers
- One or more Workstations
- A Cabling System
- Desktop Environment(s)
- Application Software
- Peripheral Devices

Novell publishes two basic versions of *NetWare* software. These differ in the speed, capacity, features, and, of course, price. Within each version, Novell has several levels from which to choose, based solely on the maximum number of concurrent users that fileserver can support. While it is possible to upgrade from one version to another, it is usually best to select one that will handle today's requirements, while also allowing for growth at least into the near future. Each computer on the network (including fileservers) must contain a network interface card (or NIC). This is the connection through which each computer shares information (via the cabling system) with the others. There are numerous manufacturers of NICs. As of recently, Novell is no longer one of them, having handed over the few types that they did market to companies that specialize in hardware. This leaves Novell free to concentrate on its forte—developing network software.

The fileservers and workstations can be any of a variety of IBM or compatible personal computers, or computers designed especially for the purpose of being network components. Here too, Novell has given other manufacturers the rights to build and market the systems that Novell manufactured in the past. In some Novell configurations, the fileserver doubles as a workstation. The fileserver contains one or more fixed drives; workstations do not require fixed drives, and in some cases even floppy drives are optional.

Most DOS application software will run on a Novell network, but some may not take full advantage of the network features. An application designed for network use will usually allow several users to access the same program and data at once, as well as interfacing with shared printers and other peripherals. Many software publishers have versions both for stand alone and for network use. Because Novell is so widely used, the network versions of application software are usually Novell compatible.

SOFTWARE

Novell *NetWare* software includes an operating system that runs on network fileservers, certain add-on utilities that run on the fileserver, software "shells" that run on workstations, and a number of command files and utilities that reside on the fileserver(s) and are executed at the workstations. *NetWare* software also comes with installation and configuration programs and diagnostic routines.

NetWare software is now available on either 1.2 megabyte diskettes (5-1/4") or 1.44 megabyte diskettes (3-1/2"). While the 1.44 megabyte drives are standard on many systems, such as IBM's PS/2 line, there are still systems where that drive type is optional.

WORKING COPIES   As with any software, you should make duplicates as working copies and keep the originals safely stored. This is especially important because certain information during the configuration of the software may make permanent changes to files on these diskettes. For years, Novell used a copy-protection scheme that required the presence of a serialized "key device" in the fileserver. In recent years this has been removed.

Use the DOS DISKCOPY utility to create a working copy of all *NetWare* program diskettes. Refer to your DOS manual for proper use of DISKCOPY. Simply copying the files on each diskette to preformatted blanks will not work, as some of the *NetWare* programs depend on the volume labels assigned to each diskette.

SOFTWARE OPTIONS   A number of versions of *NetWare* software have been published over the years. Now Novell has stratified (and simplified) their offerings. *NetWare* 2.x is currently available in a 5, 10, 50, or 100 user version. *NetWare* 3.x can be purchased for 20, 100, or 250 users. There is also a 1000 user version, although it is certainly not widely used. Within each class of *NetWare* software the only difference of each level is the number of users supported. That is to say that *NetWare* 2.2 for 5 users is functionally identical to *NetWare* 2.2 for 100 users. This allows a growing network to upgrade to a larger number of users without having to relearn the system.

Each version of *NetWare* software is written on a different "microprocessor platform." *NetWare* 2.x is designed for fileservers based on the Intel 80286 processor or above. It will not run on 8088 or 8086 based fileservers, such as the IBM XT, the AT&T 6300, or the IBM PS/2 model 30. Systems based on higher level processors in this Intel series, such as the IBM PS/2 model 70 (80386-based) or the Compaq SystemPro (80486-based), will run *NetWare* 2.x, but it will not take full advantage of the power of these systems.

NetWare 3.x is designed for the 80386 or above. It takes full advantage of the 32-bit 80386 microprocessor, making it very fast and very powerful. It is also "80486 aware." This means that it does benefit somewhat from the enhancements of the 80486 over the 80386.

In addition to speed, 3.x users have several distinct advantages. Under 2.x, the operating system is "linked" at the time of installation. Various information and parameters provided by the installer are "locked in" to the operating system. This includes fileserver name, the allocation of the RAM for various tasks, the maximum number of files that can reside on the filserver volumes, the type and configuration of NICs in the filserver, and other important information. If any of this ever requires a change, the installation program must be rerun. For many of these, the operating system must be relinked and reinstalled. In addition to being time consuming, this also means that the filserver must be temporarily taken off line.

The 3.x operating system is "dynamic." This means that changes are made on the fly, as needed. In some cases the operating system reconfigures itself, reallocating its resources to various tasks as requirements change. Other changes are made by the installer or administrator, but usually while the server is up and running.

Both versions now have what Novell calls "system fault tolerance level II." This includes the Hot Fix concept, which means that whenever data is written to disk, it is reread to make sure that there are no errors. If it is determined that the data has been written to a failed sector of the drive, the sector is permanently marked as bad and the data is redirected to an area of the disk reserved for this purpose.

An even greater degree of fault tolerance is the ability to have *mirrored disks*. Two identical hard disks are maintained by the system, with all data written to both simultaneously. If one disk fails, a complete backup is still on-line. Using disk duplexing, there are also separate hard disk controllers. If either disk or either controller fails, the system continues as usual. Transaction Tracking System (TTS) is also provided. This tracks multiple updates to data files by your application program and will cancel the last set of updates if your program is unexpectedly interrupted. As an example, if you are running an accounting package, the entry of an invoice can affect several data files. If the process is interrupted (by a power outage, for instance), the data files will no longer be properly integrated. TTS keeps up with file transactions, and if all updates are not completed, then they are all canceled.

NetWare 2.x allows both dedicated and nondedicated fileservers. A nondedicated fileserver is one that is used simultaneously as a workstation. This can slow the fileserver considerably and therefore lower overall network performance. Therefore, it is best to only use nondedicated fileservers on small networks with relatively light work loads. There is also a risk that a user could accidentally lock up, reset, or turn off a fileserver that is being used as a workstation. *NetWare* 3.x only runs in a dedicated mode.

NetWare 3.x supports higher limits than 2.x in several aspects of storage. The following is a chart showing the limits of *NetWare* 3.11 and 2.2.

	NetWare 3.x	*NetWare* 2.x
Logical Users	250	100
Concurrent open files/server	100,000	1,000
RAM capacity	4 GB	12 MB
Disk Storage Supported	32 TB	2 GB
Number of Drives per server	1024	32
Volume Size	32 TB	255 MB
Volumes per Server	64	32
Number of Drives per volume	32	1
File size	4 GB	255 MB
Directory Entries per volume	Unlimited	32,000

One other advantage of *NetWare* 3.x is the ability to allow volumes to span drives. This means that a server containing 4 drives with a capacity of 1 gigabyte each could be configured such that attached workstations would view it as having 1 drive with a capacity of 4 megabytes. This can be important for users of applications that have very large databases. It can also simplify network administration by not making users determine which volumes should contain which applications and data.

Select a version of *NetWare* software that will provide for your current needs and allow for growth. Novell does make available certain upgrades so that if you need the features of a newer *NetWare* software version, you will not have to purchase an entire new system.

FILESERVERS

The fileserver is a mass storage device that is the heart of the Novell network. It contains one or more fixed drives and shares the programs and data they contain with the attached workstations. Various output devices, including printers and plotters, may be attached to a fileserver. These devices are also shared with the workstations. While most small networks have only one fileserver, enterprise-wide networks may have dozens.

It is important to remember that while the various versions of Novell *NetWare* software are limited according to number of users, they are licensed by the fileserver. Each fileserver on a network must have its own copy of *NetWare* software. This is not only a licensing issue but a technical one as well. On multiserver networks, each copy of *NetWare* software periodically compares its serial number with those on the other servers. If the same copy is running on more than one server, a message is broadcast to all attached users reporting this copyright infringement. Until one of the conflicting servers is taken off-line, the message will be broadcast approximately once per minute.

COMPUTER TYPE   While a wide variety of DOS computers are available that may be used as fileservers, you must consider the type of *NetWare* software in use before selecting one. As stated earlier, *NetWare* 2.x requires an 80286 or above fileserver; 3.x requires 80386 or above. While some users may wish to cut expense by choosing lower-end (and at times, lower quality) workstations, the fileserver should be a dependable high-quality machine. If a workstation fails, one user is down. If the fileserver fails, it affects all users.

For extremely demanding networks, there is a new breed of systems called "superservers." These are typically based on very fast 80486s with intelligent drive controllers and high-speed memory and data paths. Some of these, such as the Tricord PowerFrame, can rival many mainframe systems in performance.

HARD DRIVES   The fileserver must contain at least one hard drive. This contains the *NetWare* system files and utilities as well as the applications software and data. The hard drive is prepared with Novell's own format routine (as opposed to DOS) as part of the installation.

Most brands of hard drives that are compatible with your fileserver will work. These include all of the popular drive interfaces--SCSI, ESDI, ST506, and IDE. Some drives have specifications (i.e., number of heads and cylinders, and number of sectors per track) that may not be directly supported by certain versions of *NetWare* software. This is particularly true with large ESDI drives (600 Meg and up) and the newer IDE drives. This can be overcome with third-party software add-ons, such as Ontrack's Disk Manager-N. But there are also special controllers that deal with the problem. Most network integrators are familiar with these potential problems. They, or the manufacturer, can let you know if a given drive/controller/*NetWare* combination will work.

One of the most common "bottlenecks" on a network is found at the hard drive. Be sure to select a drive/controller combination that will provide the performance you need. The other concern, of course, is capacity. Don't underestimate your potential needs in this area. The price of drives (per megabyte) has come down drastically over the last few years. Additional drives can be added to servers, or existing ones replaced with larger models; however, investing in sufficient storage to last at least the first few years can prevent the down-time and labor expense of expanding your server.

FILESERVER RAM   The minimum amount of memory (or RAM) depends on both the type of *NetWare* software in use and the size of your hard drive(s). The network operating system itself, of course, uses a certain amount of RAM. In addition, RAM is used for caching the hard drives. Simply put, this means that commonly used information from the drives is stored in RAM for quick access and greatly improved system speed. The larger the drive(s), the more RAM that is needed for this task. Both versions of *NetWare* software allow add-in programs to be run on the server concurrent with the operating system.

NetWare 2.x uses programs called VAPs (Value Added Process), and *NetWare* 3.x uses NLMs (NetWare Loadable Modules). Each of these take additional RAM. These add-in programs can range from simple routines that monitor the condition of the server's UPS (see below), to larger and complex routines that allow high-speed data searching or communication with non-Novell networks. It is possible that upon loading an add-in program to an existing fileserver, the server may report that there is not enough RAM or may simply perform much slower. In this case, RAM must be added.

Without taking any large add-in programs into consideration, here are simple guidelines for fileserver memory:

$$\text{Disk x .006 + OS}$$

NetWare 2.x:

> Disk is the total of the hard drives being used for *NetWare* software in this server (in megabytes).

> OS is the amount needed for the operating system. This is 1 megabyte for dedicated fileservers, and 2 megabytes for nondedicated fileservers.

> In any case, 2.x should have a minimum of 2.5 megabytes.

NetWare 3.x:

> Disk is the same as above.
> OS can only be dedicated. Allow 2 megabytes.
> In any case, 3.x should have a minimum of 4 megabytes.

If in doubt, remember that *NetWare* software will use extra RAM for more caching, and this can speed up overall performance.

UPS   An uninterruptable power supply (UPS) is strongly recommended for fileservers. This provides continuous power to the system in the event of a power outage. Because of the hashing and caching process described above, the system should be properly shut down to prevent loss or corruption of data. The UPS allows the operator time to do this. *NetWare* software provides a feature called "UPS monitoring." When used with a UPS that is designed to support this feature, the fileserver is alerted if the battery is almost drained (during prolonged power outages).The fileserver then proceeds to bring down the network in a safe manner on its own.

WORKSTATIONS

Workstations are the individual computers through which you access the network. Each workstation is assigned a unique address (via settings on its network interface card). To the user, however, *NetWare* software seems to make no distinction between workstations. In other words, the ability to access various resources on the network is determined by the user, not which workstation is being used. The only exception to this is when the administrator chooses to use *NetWare* software's ability to limit a user's allowed workstation. This means that a user can be confined to only being able to use the network when at predetermined workstations.

COMPUTER TYPES Workstations can be almost any IBM, COMPAQ, or compatible DOS computer. Typically, they should have one expansion slot available for the NIC. If there are no available slots (such as with many laptop computers), there are several types of NICs that attach externally to a parallel port. There are a few machines that may not function properly on a Novell network. This is especially true of some of the very early compatibles. Check with the manufacturer or your dealer to be sure. Novell spends a great deal of time and effort testing computers for their suitability as fileservers or workstations. These test results are available from Novell-authorized network integrators, or from Novell directly. There are many systems, however, that Novell has not tested which are still completely *NetWare* compatible.

HARD DRIVES The drives of the fileserver are made available to each workstation in a fairly transparent way. This means that accessing them is very similar to accessing drives on a stand-alone computer. A "local" hard drive can be used in a workstation but is not needed. If a hard drive is omitted, a floppy drive is used to allow DOS and the *NetWare* shell (software that communicates with the network) to be loaded. This need is eliminated with the use of certain NICs that contain a "Boot ROM" which allows this software to be loaded directly off of the fileserver.

WORKSTATION RAM The *NetWare* shell stays in memory and may require up to 64K of workstation RAM. Therefore, each workstation should have at least 64K in addition to memory needed for DOS and user applications. Generally, it is ideal to provide each workstation with 640K total RAM as a minimum. Novell does have workstation shells available that will load into memory above the 640K area, but they may not be compatible with all systems.

NETWORK INTERFACE CARDS

Network fileservers and workstations communicate with each other through network interface cards (NICs). Each computer on the network must contain a NIC. The NIC occupies one expansion slot in the computer and provides an external connection to which the network cable is attached. There are some NICs that attach outside of the workstation directly to a parallel port. Their performance may not be good, but with some workstations, it is the only option. There are several cabling schemes available, but the network cable in some way connects all of the computers on the network.

Dozens of manufacturers exist which provide NICs that are Novell compatible. At the time of installation, you need to specify which NIC will be used; *NetWare* software configures itself to communicate through the particular card selected. Within one network, all NICs must be of the same type, but not necessarily the same manufacturer. Several standards have been established, and for each standard multiple companies make their own version. Two or more networks using different types or standards of NICs may be interconnected via a process called bridging. A bridge is essentially one fileserver (or in some cases workstation) which has two or more NICs, each cabled to a different network. In addition to allowing dissimilar networks to communicate, bridging can speed overall network performance. Often a large network will be broken into two or more networks, each connected to a separate NIC in the fileserver. The only data from one network which crosses over to another is that which is required on the other network. This lowers overall network traffic on each separate segment.

A number of specifications differentiate the various NICs available for Novell networking. The main specifications to consider are discussed in the following sections.

TYPE OF CABLING Cabling is often the first consideration in selecting the type of network hardware you will use. Each type of NIC has particular cable requirements. Different cable types include broad and base band (coaxial), unshielded twisted pair (telephone wiring), shielded twisted pair (popular with IBM networks), and even fiber optic. Some NICs may allow the use of more than one type of cable.

SPEED OF TRANSMISSION The speed at which data is transmitted over the network is determined by the NIC. It is measured in bits per second. A *bit* is the smallest unit of data, represented by a 1 or 0. Cards are rated in kilobits (thousand bits) or megabits (million bits) per second. Depending on the NIC you select, your network may communicate at anywhere from 500 kilobits/second (or .5 megabits) to 100 megabits/second!

METHOD OF COLLISION CONTROL In a network environment workstations and fileservers communicate with each other over a system of cabling. Because several computers may need to access the network simultaneously, there must be some way to control traffic.

One such method is called token passing. A token is a special string of data that is sent over the network, from one computer to the next. Whichever computer has the token may "broadcast" data or data requests over the network. Each computer must wait its turn to broadcast, thus collisions of data cannot occur. This whole process happens very quickly; to the user it appears that all computers are communicating at once. ARCnet and Token-Ring are two NIC standards that use this method.

Another popular method is one in which computers monitor the network cable (or "carrier") and when no traffic is detected it broadcasts. The network monitors this process and is able to detect data collisions. When one occurs, all NICs back up a step and begin transmitting their last data over again. This method is very fast in most networks; however, in very large networks the number of collisions can increase exponentially and erode overall performance. An example of this method, known as "carrier sense multiple access with collision detection and avoidance," is the Ethernet NIC.

Ethernet (also referred to as IEEE 802.3) has been in use for many years and has possibly the largest installed base of any network standard. Most existing Ethernet uses either a multiconductor long-distance cable (thicknet), or a coax cable (thin-net). Recently a standard for running Ethernet over unshielded twisted pair was established by the IEEE. Called "10base-T," it is probably the fastest growing NIC technology on the market today.

NETWORK DISTANCE   In choosing a NIC and cabling scheme, bear in mind the total area which the network will cover. Each manufacturer publishes distance specifications for its products. With some NICs, you may have the option of using different types of cables, and/or signal boosters, to attain maximum distances. There are also products available to allow networks to be bridged across considerable distances, using fiber optics, microwave, or dedicated phone lines.

RAM SIZE   NICs have memory on them to serve as a buffer between the card and the network. This allows the NIC to transmit or receive data while the computer attends to other tasks. The larger the buffer, the faster the overall operation can be.

DATA BUS SIZE   Some NICs are designed to fit in the 8-bit data bus slot of IBM PC XTs and compatibles. These cards will also work in 286/386 level machines, but only as 8-bit cards. (This means the NIC communicates with the computer 8 bits at a time.) Most manufacturers have 16-bit versions of their cards available. These work only in 286 and above computers but speed overall network access considerably. Even if you do not use 16-bit NICs in workstations, you should use them in fileservers. There are also 32-bit NICs available for the new EISA bus computers (such as the Compaq

System Pro or the Tricord PowerFrame). These provide outstanding throughput for networks with heavy traffic.

OVERALL SPEED

The performance of a NIC depends upon the speed of transmission, the way it handles collisions, the amount of buffer memory on board, and the size of the data bus. The speed of the network can depend upon a number of factors, including speed of fileserver(s), speed of workstation(s), speed of shared hard disk(s), number of users, speed of NICs, segmentation of the network, and the nature of the applications used on the network. Therefore, it is not always advisable to buy very expensive, state-of-the-art NICs if the rest of the network is not fast enough to take full advantage of them. At the same time, don't negate the power of high-speed workstations by using excessively slow NICs.

Complete technical specifications on various NICs are available from the manufacturers or your network integrator.

Turn to Module 3 to continue the learning sequence.

Module 3
HARDWARE INSTALLATION

DESCRIPTION

After selecting the appropriate products for your Novell network, it is time to install and configure the hardware components. This includes cabling, network interface cards, fileservers, and workstations. The installation of hard drives and interface cards and the running and connecting of network cable can be a difficult job. There are numerous potential pitfalls and the job is best left to professional network installers. However if you want to undertake this yourself, keep these tips in mind:

- The cable is the lifeline of your network. When running it, be sure that it is not at risk of being damaged or becoming worn. This is especially important with certain types of network interface cards (NICs) such as Ethernet, because a broken cable can shut down the entire network.

- Stick to the exact cable specified by the manufacturer of the NICs your are using. Using the wrong cable can prevent the network from operating at all or, worse yet, cause intermittent problems that may be very difficult to trace back to the cable.

- Take extra care when fastening the connectors on the cable. A sloppy connection can cause severe problems down the road.

- Read carefully the installation instructions for the NICs before attempting to install them. Wrong switch or jumper settings can affect one workstation, or the entire network.

- If the NICs you are using have selectable node address settings (such as ARCnet), set the addresses on all cards before installing any of them. Make a record of the address of each card so that when expanding in the future you will know which addresses are still available.

- Remember that static discharge, when touching computer components, can cause costly damage.

- Use great care in handling hard drives. Even a slight jolt to the drive can cause permanent damage.

- When expanding RAM memory, be sure to use chips that are rated at sufficient speed for the computer you are using. Different manufacturers require different types of RAM.

- Verify *NetWare* compatibility for all network components. Be sure to state the version of *NetWare* software you are using. Often times a given component will operate under one version yet not under another. You can check on this through the manufacturers or through your network integrator. One of the most important responsibilities of a network integrator is to stay current on compatibility issues. Remember that while *NetWare* software is fairly simple and straightforward for most computer users, the actual installation and configuration of a network can be quite involved. It is usually best to leave this to Novell trained technicians, or at least have them available to consult. Novell authorized network integrators should have such trained personnel on their staff.

Turn to Module 4 to continue the learning sequence.

Module 4
COMPSURF & ZTEST

DESCRIPTION

The ZTEST utility thoroughly tests track 0 on fileserver hard drives, then prepares them for *NetWare* usage. The COMPSURF utility formats and performs extensive tests on all tracks of the fileserver drive(s). Both of these tests assure the drive's suitability for the network. COMPSURF also locates and marks any bad areas. ZTEST takes only minutes to run. Depending on the size of the drive, COMPSURF can take anywhere from 2 to more than 16 hours. It is possible that either utility will reject a drive that a standard DOS format would accept as usable.

APPLICATIONS

The reliability of the fileserver(s) hard drives is paramount. With stand-alone systems, a hard drive failure can result in data loss, but assuming that backups are performed regularly, this is minimal. The main problem is that the user is typically down for several hours to several days. Because a fileserver can service dozens of users, when a server drive fails, the problems and related expense can be exponentially worse.

Traditionally, Novell encouraged the use of COMPSURF on all fileserver drives. While very time consuming, it was far better to find potential problems before the drive was put into use. Today this has changed.

Most of today's drives (and in particular the larger drives that networks typically use) are much more reliable. Drive manufacturers test their products much more rigorously, and most problem areas on drives are marked at the factory. Further, both current versions of *NetWare* software now employ system fault tolerance. The Hot Fix scheme tests every block on a drive each time data is written to it. Thus it is no longer necessary to test drives with COMPSURF, but the utility is provided for those who still wish to use it.

Track 0 on fileserver drives is the most critical. If it fails, the drive cannot be used. Therefore a comprehensive test of this track is still required.

TYPICAL OPERATION

In this activity you format and perform extensive tests on your hard drive before installing Novell *NetWare* software. Because COMPSURF will destroy all data on the drive, it is important to have a complete understanding of the particular version of COMPSURF you are using. Refer to the *NetWare* installation manual for more details. Start COMPSURF according to the manual's instructions. The screen will resemble:

```
DISK  FORMATTER  and  COMPREHENSIVE  SURFACE
ANALYSIS PROGRAM (C)Copyright Novell Inc. 1983,
1984, 1985, 1986

Version: NW2.2 Date: 01 Jan 1991

**** WARNING ****

THIS  PROGRAM COMPLETELY ERASES ALL DATA ON THE
DISK

Enter today's date:
```

1. Using the MM/DD/YY format, type today's date and press **Enter**. The screen now lists all present hard drives. If the list is incorrect, your drives may be improperly installed. If you have one drive installed, the screen should resemble the following:

```
The  following  disk  drive(s)  are attached to
this PC:

1.  IBM Hard Disk "C" type 08
Select the drive to be tested.
```

CAUTION

The drive you select is not only tested, but first formatted, destroying any data on it.

2. Type the appropriate drive number. In this case, with only one drive present you would type **1**. Press **Enter**. The screen now shows:

```
Enter the interleave (1-16)
```

The interleave value determines how data is stored on the drive. The lower the number, the faster the data is written and retrieved. If, however, you use an interleave too low, your system may not be able to keep up with it, resulting in greatly impaired speed. Most systems perform best with a value of 2.

3. Type **2** and press **Enter**. Now the screen shows:

```
Enter the number of times to repeat the
regular surface analysis (0-3):
```

It is the surface analysis that takes the majority of the time spent running COMPSURF. To assure greatest dependability, it is recommended that you select three repetitions of this process. Roughly speaking, the analysis takes about 30 minutes per 10 megabytes of drive space for each repetition. Therefore, selecting three repetitions with an 80 megabyte drive may take up to 12 hours or more.

4. Type **3** and press **Enter**. The screen now asks:

```
Read the "bad block" list from the disk?
(y/n)
```

5. Type **N** and press **Enter** as COMPSURF often cannot read any existing table of defective drive areas (or bad blocks), and COMPSURF does an extensive job of finding all bad blocks. The screen now verifies the information you have entered. An example follows:

```
          Date:    01/01/91
    Disk Model:    IBM Hard DISK "C"
                   type 08
Controller type:   IBM

The disk will be FORMATTED!
The interleave = 2
The "surface" test will be repeated 3 time(s).
The existing bad block list will not be retained.

Are these entries correct? (y/n)
```

6. Type **N** to change any of the listed information or type **Y** to proceed with the format/testing.

7. Press **Enter**. For the next several hours, COMPSURF displays various information on the screen as it formats the drive and performs sequential read/write tests. Next, a random seek test begins. This runs until you interrupt it. Allow it to run an additional two to six hours, then proceed to step 8.

8. Type **S** and press **Enter**. COMPSURF responds with:

```
Do you really want to terminate the test?
```

9. Type **YY** and press **Enter**. COMPSURF asks:

```
Would you like to print the error report?
(yy/nn)
```

10. If you wish to maintain a list of all bad blocks which COMPSURF has marked, type **YY** and press **Enter**. This report could prove useful in the event that the bad block table on your drive is ever deleted. Otherwise, type **NN** and press **Enter**. COMPSURF is now complete.

11. Turn to Module 5 to continue the learning sequence.

Module 5
NET$OS
(ver 2.x)

DESCRIPTION

The heart of the Novell *NetWare* 2.x operating system is a program called NET$OS. It is an executable (.EXE) file located on the fileserver. NET$OS controls network communication, servicing requests from all attached workstations for disk I/O, network printer access, and messaging. While many of the public and console commands are the same in the two versions of *NetWare*, NET$OS differs considerably from the *NetWare* 3.x fileserver operating system (see Module 6).

On dedicated fileservers (ones which cannot be used as workstations) NET$OS is located on the first network hard drive and is loaded automatically upon booting the computer. DOS is not present in the operation of dedicated fileservers. Nondedicated fileservers usually load NET$OS from a diskette. This "fileserver boot diskette" loads DOS, then NET$OS (often called from the AUTOEXEC.BAT file). Once NET$OS is running (as a "background" operation) the fileserver returns to DOS and is usable as an extra workstation.

The NET$OS program must be generated at the time of network installation. The program exists on the Novell diskettes in a nonexecutable form. The program INSTALL.EXE links various files to create NET$OS. As part of this procedure, the installer specifies information about the hard disk controllers, NICs, and a number of fileserver parameters. INSTALL uses this input to select the correct files to link together, and to configure them. Thus NET$OS is customized for your specific installation requirements. Finally, NET$OS is installed on the fileserver hard drive by the INSTALL program (or copied to the boot diskette).

TYPICAL OPERATION

NET$OS and the related generation programs can change considerably with each release of *NetWare*. The installation of a fileserver is quite involved and requires extensive knowledge. For details on proper generation and installation of NET$OS, refer to your *NetWare* installation manuals or consult your local network integrator.

Turn to Module 6 to continue the learning sequence.

Module 6
SERVER
(ver 3.x)

DESCRIPTION

The heart of the Novell *NetWare* 3.x operating system is a program named SERVER. It is an executable (.EXE) file located on the fileserver. SERVER is a multitasking core into which a number of programs are loaded. These include DSK programs which interface with hard drive controllers, LAN programs which interface with the fileserver NIC(s), and NLMs or *NetWare* Loadable Modules which do just about everything that the 3.x operating system provides.

Combined with these, SERVER controls network communication, servicing requests from all attached workstations for disk I/O, network printer access, and messaging. While many of the public and console commands are the same in the two versions of *NetWare*, SERVER and its loadable components differ considerably from the *NetWare* 2.x fileserver operating system (see Module 5).

SERVER operates in a dynamic fashion. This means that its configuration can and does change while it is running. For instance, external hard drives can be removed, replaced, and reconfigured without the fileserver ever being DOWNed (or taken off line). The configuration of NICs can likewise be modified in certain ways while the fileserver is up. And SERVER is constantly monitoring itself and changing internal parameters as needed to provide optimum operation.

Novell currently has available dozens of NLMs. They also encourage third party development of these programs. They range in application from high-speed data access routines to communication programs that allow dissimilar or remote system to integrate with the 3.x fileserver. All of these NLMs can be loaded and unloaded as required while the fileserver remains running.

SERVER truly takes advantage of the 80386 microprocessor and even benefits to a certain extent from the 80486. It is because of this advanced platform that it was designed with the aforementioned multitasking dynamic capabilities. The one 2.x feature that SERVER does not provide is the ability to run the fileserver in a nondedicated mode. However, even under 2.x this is not advised, as there are performance and risk concerns.

TYPICAL OPERATION

The use of SERVER and the related loadable programs can change with each release of *NetWare*. The installation of a fileserver is quite involved and requires extensive knowledge. For details on proper installation and configuration of the 3.x fileserver operating systems, refer to your *NetWare* installation manuals, or consult your local network integrator.

Turn to Module 7 to continue the learning sequence.

Module 7
WORKSTATION SHELLS
(ver 2.x and 3.x)

DESCRIPTION

The only part of *NetWare* that must reside on workstations are two programs called collectively the "workstation shell." When a workstation is booted with DOS, the appropriate shell programs must be loaded before you can access the network (see Booting the System, Module 8). The shell controls workstation communication (through the network interface card, or NIC) with the network.

The shell consists of IPX and NET. Actually the NET program also includes a single digit to indicate the version of DOS for which it was written. For example, DOS 3.x workstations use NET3; DOS 5.x uses NET5. IPX communicates with the NIC at all times. NET provides the actual workstation services and communicates with IPX.

IPX must be custom generated, similar to NET$OS (Module 5). This is done with WSGEN, found on the *NetWare* installation diskettes. WSGEN links and configures into IPX a driver that is written especially for the type of NIC being used in the workstation. *NetWare* includes a number of such drivers for such popular NICs as Ethernet, Token Ring, and ARCnet. But many manufacturers of NICs have written their own drivers. In some cases they are needed because their NICs are proprietary and will not work with the Novell-provided drivers. In other cases they simply offer better performance. WSGEN requests the appropriate drive be loaded and then asks for configuration information. Depending on the NIC, this can include Interrupt Number, Base I/O Address, and others. Refer to the instruction manual for detailed instructions for a particular NIC.

TYPICAL OPERATION

Workstation shells and the related generation programs change considerably with each version of *NetWare*. For details on proper generation and installation of these shells, refer to your *NetWare* installation manual or consult a local network integrator.

Turn to Module 8 to continue the learning sequence.

Module 8
BOOTING THE SYSTEM
(ver 2.x and 3.x)

DESCRIPTION

Turning on a fully installed network and bringing it on-line is a process referred to as *booting the system*. Before doing this, you should complete modules 1 through 7. The fileserver(s) must be booted prior to any workstations being turned on. Many network administrators choose to leave the fileserver always booted and available to the network. Others choose to bring down the fileserver each night and reboot it each morning. Workstations are turned on and booted onto the network each day, though they should only be logged in to the network (see Module 48) when in use.

Booting 2.x fileservers essentially consists of turning on the computer and loading the NET$OS program. Dedicated fileservers (ones that do not double as workstations) have NET$OS on their first hard drive. The computer is turned on with the floppy drive open, and a system program called the "cold boot loader" loads and starts NET$OS. Nondedicated fileservers load NET$OS from a diskette (referred to as the "fileserver boot diskette"). The computer is turned on with the boot diskette in drive A. DOS loads from the diskette, then an AUTOEXEC.BAT file loads NET$OS. Finally, with NET$OS running as a background task, the fileserver returns to a DOS prompt, ready to use as a workstation. Use CONSOLE and DOS (Modules 23 and 31) to toggle between the fileserver and workstation modes.

To boot 3.x fileservers, turn on the system and boot DOS. Depending on how the fileserver was installed, this is either a DOS partition on the first fileserver hard drive or a DOS-bootable diskette. When DOS is booted, run SERVER (typically done by the AUTOEXEC.BAT file on the bootup drive). Now the fileserver must load at least one hard drive controller drive (this program will have a .DSK extension) and mount at least the first volume (always called SYS). The fileserver name is assigned, a unique network number is assigned, and a NIC driver is loaded. These drivers have the extension .LAN. Each driver that is loaded must include configuration information. Finally, the internal network (IPX) is bound to the LAN driver. This all sounds complicated, and it can be. Fortunately, these commands are all stored in the AUTOEXEC.NCF file and should execute automatically. Booting workstations requires turning on the computer, booting DOS, and loading the appropriate workstation shell. DOS may be booted from a hard drive or from floppy drive A. The shell must be configured for the network interface card in use. For a more detailed explanation of the workstation shell, see Module 7. Once the shell (IPX.COM and NETx.COM) is running, the first network drive will be available. On workstations running DOS 3.x or above this will usually be drive F. From this drive, you can log in to the network.

An increasingly popular network computer is the *diskless* workstation. This is a computer with memory, microprocessor, screen, and keyboard, but without hard or floppy drives. The built-in network interface card contains a permanent memory chip (called the *boot ROM*) that contains the workstation shell. To boot the diskless workstation, simply turn it on. DOS is loaded from the fileserver over the network.

Bringing a workstation down simply requires logging out (Module 49) and turning off the computer. At the fileserver, use DOWN (Module 32) to close any open files and the disk cache, and turn off the computer. It is important to make sure that all users have logged out (or at least exited any application) before using DOWN, and it is vital that you run DOWN before powering off or resetting the fileserver.

TYPICAL OPERATION

In this activity you boot the network, starting with the fileserver.

1. With drive A open, turn on the fileserver. The fileserver screen shows various information about the drive(s) that are being mounted and cached, the copyright message, and the date and time. When the fileserver is fully booted, the screen displays the console prompt — :. Some fileservers may be configured to load MONITOR. Now the workstations can be booted.

2. Turn on the workstation and boot DOS. If the workstation has a hard drive, it probably contains DOS. Floppy drive systems will need a bootable DOS diskette in drive A. Diskless workstations will load DOS from the fileserver. If you are not using a diskless workstation, execute the workstation shell (see Module 7). Floppy drive machines will contain the shell on the bootable DOS diskette. On hard drive machines, change to the directory containing the shell. When you see the DOS prompt, continue to step 3.

3. Type **IPX** and press **Enter**. The screen displays information concerning the NIC configuration. Then type **NETx** (depending on your DOS version; DOS 3.x, for instance, uses NET3) and press **Enter**. The screen resembles the following:

```
A>NET3
Advanced NetWare V2.01-3 Workstation Shell for PC DOS V3.x
Copyright (c) by Novell, Inc. 1983, 1987

LAN Option: Novell RX-Net

Attached to server MAIN
Tuesday, January 1, 1991   3:55:07 pm


A>
```

Next, you create the necessary files and directories needed to continue the learning sequence. A basic knowledge of DOS is helpful for these steps. You will probably need the assistance of the network administrator to set up the required network security parameters.

4. Type **F:** and press **Enter**.

5. Type **LOGIN** and press **Enter**.

6. Type your name and press **Enter**.

7. Type your password and press **Enter**.

8. Type **MD\INN** and press **Enter**.

9. Type **CD\INN** and press **Enter**.

10. Type **COPY CON TEST.TXT** and press **Enter**. The cursor will return to the left edge of the screen.

11. Type **THIS IS A TEST** and press **Enter**. The cursor again returns to the edge.

12. Type **Ctrl-Z** and press **Enter**.

13. Repeat steps 10-12 using the following filenames. For example, the next file you need to create is REPORT.TXT. Insert REPORT.TXT where you typed TEST.TXT in step 10.

    REPORT.TXT
    SALES.LET
    TEST.PRN
    321.EXE

14. Type **COPY CON START.BAT** and press **Enter**.

15. Type **DIR** and press **Enter**. This will cause a directory listing to be displayed each time this batch file is used.

16. Type **Ctrl-Z** and press **Enter**.

17. Repeat steps 14-16 using the filename GO.BAT.

Next you create two users that are needed throughout the learning sequence.

18. Type **SYSCON** and press **Enter**.

19. Use the Down Arrow to highlight "User Information" and press **Enter**.

20. Press the **Insert** key.

21. Type **FRED** and press **Enter**.

22. Press **Enter**.

23. Use the Down Arrow to highlight "Security Equivalences" and press **Enter**.

24. Use the Down Arrow to highlight "SUPERVISOR" and press **Enter**.

25. Press the **Esc** key.

26. Use the Up Arrow to highlight "Password" and press **Enter**.

27. Type **SUNSHINE** and press **Enter**.

28. Press the **Esc** key.

29. Repeat steps 18-28 using the username BOB.

30. Press the **Esc** key twice to exit SYSCON.

31. Turn to Module 48 to continue the learning sequence.

Module 9
ATOTAL
(ver 2.x and 3.x)

DESCRIPTION

ATOTAL is a system command valid only on networks in which the "accounting" feature has been activated (this is accomplished with SYSCON, Module 86). ATOTAL totals various network services and lists the summaries on the screen. The report includes blocks written and read, connection time by all users, disk storage (in blocks * days), and total number of service requests. You can obtain a hard copy of this report by redirecting screen output to a printer or text file by using the DOS > PRN or > FILENAME command after ATOTAL.

APPLICATIONS

NetWare "accounting" allows administrators to break down overall network usage among users or groups. This is useful in billing different departments for network use, as well as projecting future network needs and expansion. ATOTAL helps determine billing rates by reporting total network usage. For more information on accounting see SYSCON, Module 86.

TYPICAL OPERATION

In this activity you print a report of total network usage. Begin at the DOS prompt of a logged-in workstation.

1. To send the report to a local printer, ensure that the local printer port is not redirected to the network—type **ENDCAP** and press **Enter**. To direct the report to a network printer queue (in this case a queue called "LASER" on the default server), type **CAPTURE Q=LASER** and press **Enter**. ENDCAP and CAPTURE are covered in modules 36 and 14.

2. Type **ATOTAL > PRN** and press **Enter**.

3. Turn to Module 63 to continue the learning sequence.

Module 10
ATTACH
(ver 2.x and 3.x)

DESCRIPTION

The public command ATTACH establishes a connection to a specified fileserver on multiserver networks. The fileserver's resources are made available to you (within the constraints of your user rights as established by SYSCON; see Module 86). ATTACH is similar to LOGIN (see Module 48) except that it is only used after you have logged in to a different fileserver. In other words, you must log in to a server before you can ATTACH to additional servers. Also, ATTACH does not execute a login script (see Module 48).

APPLICATIONS

On multiserver networks you can have access to several fileservers at the same time. Use LOGIN to establish the first fileserver connection, then use ATTACH to establish additional connections. Once ATTACHed to a server, you must use the MAP command (Module 52) before you can access the server's volumes.

TYPICAL OPERATION

This activity is only valid on networks with more than one fileserver. In this activity you LOGIN to your default server, then ATTACH to a second fileserver. This activity assumes a second fileserver named ACCT. Any other valid fileserver name can be substituted. Begin at the DOS prompt of a logged-in workstation.

1. LOGIN to the default server (see Module 51).
2. Type **ATTACH ACCT** and press **Enter**.
3. Type your username and press **Enter**.
4. If prompted, type your password and press **Enter**. (If you do not have one, you will not be prompted for one.)

You now have access to both the default and the ACCT fileservers. Use LOGOUT (see Module 49) to detach from either or both of these fileservers.

5. Turn to Module 92 to continue the learning sequence.

Module 11
BINDFIX
(ver 2.x and 3.x)

DESCRIPTION

The BINDFIX rebuilds certain system files to correct certain *NetWare* errors. It should only be used by knowledgeable network administrators.

Information concerning valid users, groups, fileservers, accounting, and print queues is stored in hidden files, collectively called the network *bindery*. If these files are ever corrupted, you may encounter abnormal errors. These will usually concern the inability of even supervisors to modify user or group information or unknown fileserver errors. On the fileserver console they may specifically be referred to as bindery problems. BINDFIX can usually repair such problems by rebuilding the bindery. BINDFIX will first make backup copies of the bindery in the SYS:SYSTEM directory. In the event of an unsuccessful attempt to BINDFIX, these backup files are used by BINDREST (see Module 12) to restore the old bindery. During the BINDFIX process certain functions will not be available to users; the administrator may want to run this process with all users logged out.

NOTE
The backup bindery files are called NET$BVAL.OLD and NET$BIND.OLD. They are placed in the SYS:SYSTEM directory. After running BINDFIX, it is important not to delete these files until you are sure that the bindery has been successfully rebuilt. Without these files, BINDREST cannot restore the bindery to its previous condition. A somewhat corrupted bindery is better than a completely corrupted bindery!

In the event BINDFIX encounters user or trustee rights which should be deleted, you are prompted for permission to do so. When finished, BINDFIX reports:

```
Bindery check successfully completed.
Please delete the files NET$BIND.OLD and NET$BVAL.OLD after
you have verified the reconstructed bindery.
```

You verify the new bindery by logging in and out under various usernames, printing to different print queues, and testing for appropriate trustee rights in different directories. In the event that BINDFIX is not able to reconstruct the bindery, it displays:

```
Bindery check NOT successfully completed.
```

If this occurs, or if the workstation or fileserver is interrupted during the BINDFIX process, use BINDREST (see Module 12) immediately to restore the old bindery.

APPLICATIONS

In the event of bindery corruption, you can experience problems in executing basic *NetWare* operations. These problems can become steadily worse! Use BINDFIX to rebuild the bindery and restore normal network use. BINDFIX will also perform certain "housekeeping" tasks, bringing the binderies up to date for the current network setup.

TYPICAL OPERATION

It is best *not* to run BINDFIX unless network errors indicate its necessity. If you have encountered such a need, perform the following steps. Begin at the DOS prompt of a logged-in workstation.

1. Type **BINDFIX** and press **Enter**. Your display shows a list of tasks as BINDFIX performs them. The screen resembles this:

```
F> BINDFIX

Rebuilding Bindery. Please wait.

Checking object's property lists.
Checking properties to see if they are in an object property list.
Checking objects for back-link property.
Checking set consistency and compacting sets.
Checking properties for proper order.
Checking user objects for standard properties.
Checking group objects for standard properties.
Checking links between users and groups for consistency.

Delete mail directories of users that no longer exist? (y/n):
```

2. To remove the mail directories and their contents for any users that have been removed from the network, type **Y** and press **Enter**. BINDFIX will delete any such directories, then check to see if there are any users that do not have mail directories. The screen continues like this:

```
Checking for mail directories of users that no longer exist.
Checking for users that do not have mail directories.

Delete trustee rights for users that no longer exist? (y/n):
```

3. To delete from the new bindery any rights assignments from users that have been removed from the network, type **Y** and press **Enter**.
4. Turn to Module 12 to continue the learning sequence.

Module 12
BINDREST
(ver 2.x and 3.x)

DESCRIPTION

BINDREST restores the old bindery in the event that a newly constructed bindery is incomplete or otherwise unusable. For a complete explanation of the binderies see BINDFIX, Module 11. BINDREST uses two files that BINDFIX creates prior to rebuilding the bindery. These are:

SYS:SYSTEM\NET$BIND.OLD

SYS:SYSTEM\NET$BVAL.OLD

If these files have been deleted, BINDREST will not work.

APPLICATIONS

It is unlikely that you will need to rebuild the bindery. In the event you do, BINDFIX usually does so successfully. If, however, BINDFIX fails, it is vital that you use BINDREST to restore the old bindery. Though it may have flaws, it is better than a completely corrupted bindery!

TYPICAL OPERATION

This activity, like the Typical Operation section of BINDFIX, should be read but not actually performed unless you have an actual need to restore an old bindery. Begin at the DOS prompt of a logged-in workstation.

1. Type **BINDREST** and press **Enter**.

Assuming that the backup files are present in the SYS:SYSTEM directory, the old bindery will be restored.

2. Turn to Module 9 to continue the learning sequence.

Module 13
BROADCAST
(ver 2.x and 3.x)

DESCRIPTION

BROADCAST is a console command similar to SEND (see Module 79). You follow the command by a message, not enclosed in quotes, up to 60 characters in length. The message is normally sent to all logged-in (or attached) workstations immediately. Optionally, you can BROADCAST a message to selected users, but you must specify their connection number rather than their username. As with the SEND command, Ctrl-Enter clears the message from your workstation. Users may block their workstations from receiving messages with the CASTOFF command (Module 15).

Users who have dialed in remotely to a network using Novell NACS (*NetWare* Asynchronous Communication Software), PC Anywhere, Carbon Copy, or similar third party software or who are using full-screen graphics software such as Lotus Allways may experience problems when a message is BROADCAST to them. The message will not appear but can lock up their workstation. If the user thinks to try Ctrl-Enter, it may resolve the problem. But for the most part such users should use CASTOFF to prevent such problems from occurring. Fortunately, applications publishers are already reacting to such problems. Microsoft's Windows 3.0, for instance, uses full-screen graphics but intercepts *NetWare* messages and displays them harmlessly.

APPLICATIONS

Use BROADCAST to quickly send messages to all current users. This can be used by network administrators to issue global instructions such as DO NOT USE THE LASER PRINTER or LOGOUT ASAP.

TYPICAL OPERATION

In this activity you BROADCAST a message to all users currently logged in or attached to the fileserver. Begin at the : prompt of your fileserver.

1. Type **BROADCAST LOGOUT BY 5:00** and press **Enter**.
2. Turn to Module 18 to continue the learning sequence.

Module 14
CAPTURE
(ver 2.x and 3.x)

DESCRIPTION

CAPTURE is a public command which redirects subsequent printer output to the specified print queue or to a specified file. During the CAPTURE process, output is temporarily stored in a *spool file*. This file is then transferred in its entirety to the queue.

Under DOS 2.X, the output is accumulated until you issue the ENDCAP command. DOS 3.X and above automatically sends the spooled output to the print queue when you exit the application. Either way, the spool file is automatically deleted after being processed by the queue. There are 19 flags that affect the way in which CAPTUREd output is printed. Many of them are similar to the flags used with NPRINT (see Module 60). You may use the full name or the abbreviation of each one. (If you do not use flags, the defaults mentioned in the following descriptions are used.)

A (Autoendcap)	There are no parameters. This flag forces an ENDCAP (see Module 36) upon exiting an application. CAPTUREd output is then transferred to the specified queue (see Q flag) and printed. The default is Autoendcap enabled.
B= (Banner=)	The parameter is text, which can be up to twelve characters and is printed on the banner page preceding the printout. The default is LST:.
C= (Copies=)	The parameter is the number of copies to print. The allowed range is 0 to 255. The default is 1.
CR= (Create=)	The parameter is a filename which can be preceded with a full path. When you use this flag, output is saved to the given filename as well as to the spool file. Thus, after the spool file is printed, additional printouts can be obtained by NPRINTing the CREATEd file. The default is to not create an output file. Note: If a fileserver is specified in the path of the filename to be CREATEd, it overrides any fileserver name specified with the S flag. The CAPTUREd output is sent to the selected printer number attached to the fileserver indicated by the CREATE flag.

F= (Forms=)

The parameter is a number which specifies the type of form on which the file should be printed. The allowed range is 0 to 255. Just before printing the file, the fileserver to which the target printer is attached verifies that the requested form number is the same as the last one used on that printer. If not, a message is displayed asking that the appropriate form type be loaded. Once an operator has loaded the correct form, printing is resumed by typing START PRINTER at the fileserver console and pressing Enter. The assignment of form type to form numbers is arbitrary. A list of available forms and their corresponding numbers should be established through PRINTDEF and provided to all users.

FF (Form Feed)

There are no parameters. This flag restores the issuance of automatic form feeds. It counteracts the NFF flag if it was used on a previous CAPTURE command. The default is to form feed.

J= (Job=)

The parameter is the name of the print job configuration you wish to use. Predefined configurations eliminate the need to specify many of the flags used with CAPTURE. For a complete explanation of print job configurations, see PRINTCON in Module 65. The default is to not use a predefined configuration.

K (Keep)

There are no parameters. CAPTUREd output is held in a temporary spool file and not transferred to a print queue until the TI flag or the ENDCAP command forces such a transfer. If your workstation is turned off, reset, or otherwise detached from the network before spooled output has been placed in a print queue, the output is lost. The Keep flag prevents such a loss by queuing any partial output accumulated at the time of an unexpected detachment. The default is Keep disabled.

L= (Local=)

The parameter is a single-digit number indicating the local parallel printer port (LPT1: through LPT3:) which is to be redirected by the CAPTURE command. The range is 1 to 3. The default is 1.

NA (NoAutoendcap)

There are no parameters. An ENDCAP command (see Module 36) is normally issued automatically when you exit (or enter) an application. This causes CAPTUREd output to be transferred to the specified print queue and to begin printing. The NA flag disables this action. Output remains spooled until

	you manually issue the ENDCAP command. The default is NoAutoendcap disabled.
NAME=	The parameter is the username you wish to have printed on the banner page. Obviously, this flag is not valid when the NB flag is used. The default is to print your current username.
NB (No Banner)	There are no parameters. Include this flag to suppress the printing of a banner page before the file is printed. The default is to print banner pages.
NFF (No Form Feed)	There are no parameters. If the file being printed contains form feed commands, include this command to suppress additional automatic form feeds. The default is automatic form feeds.
NT (No Tabs)	There are no parameters. This flag causes tab characters to be ignored when printing the CAPTUREd file. The default is to not ignore tabs.
Q= (Queue=)	The parameter is the name of the print queue you want to receive this print job. The default is the first queue on the specified printer. If no printer, fileserver, and queue are specified, the print job is sent to the current default server, printer 0, and queue PRINTQ_0.
S= (Server=)	The parameter is a text string naming any fileserver. This server is the target for the files to be printed. If the server has more than one printer attached, you can select one with the P flag or allow the default of 0. The server chosen does not have to be one to which you are currently logged in or attached. *NetWare* will temporarily log in to that server, print the files, and log back out. This procedure uses the GUEST username. If a password has been assigned to GUEST, you are prompted to enter it. If the GUEST username has been deleted, you are given the opportunity to log in using any other valid username. The default is the fileserver to which you are currently logged.
SH (Show)	There are no parameters. This flag causes the CAPTURE command to simply list how flag values are currently set. Use it only with no other flags. The default is to not show.
T= (Tabs=)	The parameter is the number of columns which separate the tabs in the files to be printed. The range is 0 to 18. If a file is generated by an application which does not format tabs prior to printing, this flag tells *NetWare* how to interpret the file. The default is 8.

TI= (Timeout=)   The parameter is a number of seconds to wait after output to the spool file has ceased before issuing an automatic ENDCAP. The range is 0 to 1000. Without this flag or with a value of 0, you must exit an application every time you want spooled output to be printed. As this can be quite an inconvenience, use this flag with a value of 10 or 15 seconds to cause timely automatic printouts. Setting the value to 0 seconds disables automatic ENDCAPs. The default is no timeouts.

APPLICATIONS

Some software applications, such as WordPerfect 5.x or Microsoft Windows 3.x are designed with the ability to send output directly to network printers. When using other programs, issuing the CAPTURE command prior to entering the application can allow the easy transfer of output to any printer attached to any available fileserver.

TYPICAL OPERATION

In this activity, you redirect printouts from LPT1: on your workstation to a queue named LASER on the default fileserver. Assuming you do not have a queue by that name, substitute any valid queue name. At the DOS prompt of a logged-in workstation:

1. Type **CAPTURE L=1 Q=LASER** and press **Enter**.

2. Now enter any application and produce printouts as you normally would, directing them to LPT1:. They are stored in a temporary spool file. The screen should resemble the following:

```
F:\>CAPTURE L=1 Q=LASER
Device LPT1: re-routed to queue LASER on server MAIN.

F:\>
```

3. Exit the application. The output from your application now begins to print on the selected network printer.

   Now display the current status of the CAPTURE flags.

4. Type **CAPTURE SH** and press **Enter**.

   Next use the TI flag to allow immediate printouts while in the application. Also produce 2 copies of the output.

5. Type **CAPTURE TI=15 C=2** and press **Enter**. Notice the display:

```
F:\>CAPTURE TI=15 C=2
Device LPT1: re-routed to printer 2 on server MAIN.

F:\>
```

The L and P flags remain set as in step 1 until they are specifically reset in a CAPTURE command.

6. Reenter your application and produce a printout. This time the printing begins 15 seconds later.

7. Exit your application.

8. Turn to Module 36 to continue the learning sequence.

Module 15
CASTOFF
(ver 2.x and 3.x)

DESCRIPTION

CASTOFF is a public command which disables your workstation from receiving messages. Messages are sent to you from other workstations or a fileserver (see SEND, Module 79, BROADCAST, Module 13). The following flags can be used with CASTOFF, although two of them are redundant. You can use the full names or the abbreviations. If you use a flag, follow the command CASTOFF with a forward slash (/), followed by the flag.

A (All)   This flag prevents all messages (from workstations or fileservers) from being received.

S (Stations)   This flag blocks messages from other workstations only. Messages sent from a fileserver console are still received. This is the same as using CASTOFF without flags.

C (Console)   This flag has the same effect as the All flag.

Use the CASTON command to reenable message receiving (see Module 16).

APPLICATIONS

When involved in an application during which you do not wish to be disturbed, use CASTOFF to prevent messages from being received and displayed on your screen. Because messaging is one of the advantages of a local area network, some network administrators may ask users not to use this command.

Users who have dialed in remotely to a network using Novell NACS (NetWare Asynchronous Communication Software), PC Anywhere, Carbon Copy, or similar third-party software or who are using full-screen graphics software such as Lotus Allways may experience problems when a message is BROADCAST to them. The message will not appear but can lock up their workstation. If the user thinks to try Ctrl-Enter, it may resolve the problem. But for the most part such users should use CASTOFF to prevent such problems from occurring. Fortunately, applications publishers are already reacting to such problems. Microsoft's Windows 3.0, for instance, uses full-screen graphics but intercepts *NetWare* messages and displays them harmlessly.

TYPICAL OPERATION

In this activity you disable your workstation's ability to receive messages from other workstations. Next you verify CASTOFF's effectiveness by attempting to SEND yourself a message (see Module 79). This example assumes your username to be Fred. Substitute your actual username where you see Fred. Begin at the DOS prompt of a logged-in workstation.

1. Type **CASTOFF S** and press **Enter**. Note the display:

```
F:\>CASTOFF S
Broadcasts from other stations will now be rejected.

F:\>
```

2. Type **SEND "HI THERE!" TO FRED** and press **Enter**. The screen resembles this:

```
F:\>SEND "HI THERE!" TO FRED
Message NOT sent to MAIN/FRED (station 6).

F:\>
```

3. Turn to Module 16 to continue the learning sequence.

Module 16
CASTON
(ver 2.x and 3.x)

DESCRIPTION

The public command CASTON negates the effects of CASTOFF (see Module 15). It fully restores the ability for your workstation to receive messages. CASTON uses no flags.

APPLICATIONS

Use CASTON to counteract the effects of the CASTOFF command.

TYPICAL OPERATION

This activity assumes you have just completed the CASTOFF operation in Module 15. You issue the CASTON command, then SEND yourself a message (see Module 79) to verify that CASTOFF has been negated. Substitute your username where you see Fred. Begin at the DOS prompt of a logged-in workstation.

1. Type **CASTON** and press **Enter**.

```
F:\>CASTON
Broadcast messages from the console and other stations will now be accepted.

F:\>
```

2. Type **SEND "HI THERE!" TO FRED** and press **Enter**.

```
F:\>SEND "HI THERE!" TO FRED
Message sent to MAIN/FRED (station 6).

F:\>
```

3. Turn to Module 87 to continue the learning sequence.

Module 17
CHKVOL
(ver 2.x and 3.x)

DESCRIPTION

The public command CHKVOL is essentially *NetWare*'s version of the DOS CHKDSK command but they are not interchangeable. CHKVOL reports the total amount of disk space allotted to given volumes, as well as how much space is currently available. It also tells you how much disk space is still available to you as a user (the network administrator can limit the amount of storage for any given user—see SYSCON, Module 86). The command can be followed by server name, volume names, and drive names, which can include the DOS wild cards, "*" and "?". The CHKVOL provides some of the same information as VOLINFO (see Module 91).

Because of the different way *NetWare* 3.x manages deleted files (see Salvage, Module 77), as well as the way it dynamically allocates fileserver resources (such as the maximum number of directory entries allowed on each volume), the information differs for the two versions of *NetWare*.

Information reported by CHKVOL:

NetWare 2.x

Total volume space
Space currently in use by files
Space remaining on volume
Space available to you
Directory entries available

NOTE
The number of directory entries under 2.x is determined at the time of volume creation. Each directory and file uses one; Macintosh files use two.

NetWare 3.x

Total volume space
Space currently in use by files
Space in use by deleted files not yet purged
Space available from deleted files

Space remaining on volume
Space available to you

NOTE

NetWare 3.x does not put a predetermined limit on the number of directory entries.

APPLICATIONS

Use CHKVOL to find out various information about the storage capacity of *NetWare* volumes.

TYPICAL OPERATION

In this activity you determine the available volume space for the current default volume. This screen is from a fileserver running *NetWare* 3.x. Begin at the DOS prompt of a logged-in workstation.

1. Type **CHKVOL** and press **Enter**. Note the display is similar to the following:

```
F:\>CHKVOL

Statistics for fixed volume MAIN/SYS:

Total volume space:                         660,000  K Bytes
Space used by files:                        324,500  K Bytes
Space in use by deleted files:              184,440  K Bytes
Space available from deleted files:         184,440  K Bytes
Space remaining on volume:                  335,500  K Bytes
Space available to USER:                     34,143  K Bytes

F:\>
```

2. Turn to Module 76 to continue the learning sequence.

Module 18
CLEAR MESSAGE
(ver 2.x)

DESCRIPTION

CLEAR MESSAGE is a console command that clears a message (as sent by SEND, Module 79) from the console screen. The console command OFF (see Module 62) clears the message, but also the entire screen.

APPLICATIONS

Use CLEAR MESSAGE to eliminate messages from the console screen after reading them. This is particularly useful when using full screen console utilities such as MONITOR (Module 55) as the utility continues to run after the message is cleared.

TYPICAL OPERATION

In this activity you clear the message "PRINTER 0 IS BROKEN!" which you sent in Module 79, SEND. Begin at the : prompt of your fileserver.

1. Type **CLEAR MESSAGE** and press **Enter**. The message at the bottom of the screen disappears.
2. Turn to Module 25 to continue the learning sequence.

Module 19
CLEAR STATION
(ver 2.x and 3.x)

DESCRIPTION

The console command CLEAR STATION closes all files in use by the specified station. The station is essentially "knocked off" or logged out of the fileserver and loses access to any of that fileserver's resources. You follow the command by the station number of the workstation to be cleared. The range is 1 and up. If you do not know the proper workstation, use the MONITOR command, Module 55.

APPLICATIONS

Use CLEAR STATION to force the closure of files in use by a given workstation and clear its connection to the fileserver. This is commonly used when the workstation cannot log out as usual. It must be used with caution. Any files that are open at the time will be immediately closed. This could cause a loss of data integrity if the workstation was in certain applications.

Under *NetWare* 3.x, stations can also be cleared using the MONITOR NLM (Module 6) either at the fileserver, or from a workstation running RCONSOLE (Module 72).

TYPICAL OPERATION

In this activity you close all files and cease fileserver communication with workstation number 3. This exercise should only be tried if you are sure that this workstation is not in the middle of an application! Begin at the : prompt of your fileserver.

1. Type **CLEAR STATION 3** and press **Enter**.

2. Station 3 sees the following error:

```
F:\>

Network Error on Server MAIN:Connection no longer valid.
Abort, Retry?
```

3. Turn to Module 26 to continue the learning sequence.

Module 20
COLORPAL
(ver 2.x and 3.x)

DESCRIPTION

NetWare has a number of menu-driven utilities, as well as the facility for users to create their own menus to drive application software. These menus are by default presented in blue, yellow, and white. The menu driven utility COLORPAL allows you to modify the color that all *NetWare* menus use, along with the colors used by *NetWare* help screens, error messages, and alerts. They can be modified for individual users or for everyone attached to the network.

The information that determines menu colors is stored in a hidden system file called IBM$RUN.OVL or CMPQ$RUN.OVL which supports IBM compatible or Compaq workstations, respectively. The Compaq version of this file is actually intended for the earlier pre-VGA Compaq computers. The PCs currently being shipped by Compaq use a graphics standard very similar to that of IBM. This .OVL file is located in the SYS:PUBLIC directory. Whenever a user runs a menu, *NetWare* searches for a file by this name and presents the menu in the colors specified.

Because of the ability to map the order in which directories are searched using the MAP command (see Module 56), a user can create a copy of this .OVL file and place it in a directory with a lower search drive number mapped to it than the SYS:PUBLIC directory, thereby giving the new copy a higher search priority. This way, *NetWare* will find this copied file and use its parameters instead of those of the original one. By this method an administrator can set up default color for all users but modify them for individual needs. To create additional copies of the .OVL file, simply run COLORPAL from a directory other than SYS:PUBLIC. If COLORPAL does not find the .OVL file in the current directory, it makes a duplicate of the existing file, which you can then modify.

COLORPAL allows you to define a number of "color palettes," each defining five different "color attributes." The five attributes include:

Background Normal

Background Reverse

Foreground Intense

Foreground Normal

Foreground Reverse

There are five built-in color palettes, each with its own default purpose. They are:

Palette	*Purpose*
0	Menus and text
1	Main headers and screen background
2	Help screens
3	Error messages
4	Alerts

Additional palettes can be defined for use within user-created menus (see Module 53).

NetWare detects the type of display in use by a given workstation. If it is a color system, the defined colors are used; if it is a TTL or VGA monochrome (the most common types), then the colors are not used. There are certain displays, however, that "confuse" *NetWare*. These include the older Compaq composite monochrome. To *NetWare* they appear to be a color system. When menus are displayed in certain color on such displays, they appear in various shades of monochrome. Certain combinations make it difficult or impossible to read the screen. This is why the alternate file CMPQ$RUN.OVL is provided. Workstations that require this approach need to notify the workstation shell. This is accomplished via the SHELL.CFG file located in the boot directory of the workstation. For these types of systems, the file should include the statement **SHORT MACHINE TYPE = CPQ**.

Upon entering the COLORPAL menu driven utility, a list of defined color palettes is displayed. As noted above, this will always include at least five choices. You can select one or use the Insert key to create a new one. You are presented with a list of five attributes. For each one you can select from a list of colors—16 choices for each foreground attribute and 8 choices for the backgrounds.

APPLICATIONS

Use COLORPAL to customize the color *NetWare* uses. You can modify the color set for various types of screens. These customizations can affect everyone or select users. Also use COLORPAL to eliminate problems with certain types of displays.

TYPICAL OPERATION

In this activity, view (but don't change) the master color setup for your default fileserver. To view the master setup, you first change your default directory to SYS:PUBLIC. Start at the DOS prompt of a logged-in workstation.

1. Type **CD\PUBLIC** and press **Enter**. Note the display.
2. Type **COLORPAL** and press **Enter**.
3. Using the Up Arrow, Down Arrow, Enter, and Esc keys, view the colors currently set for the various attributes of the different palettes.
4. A typical screen resembles this:

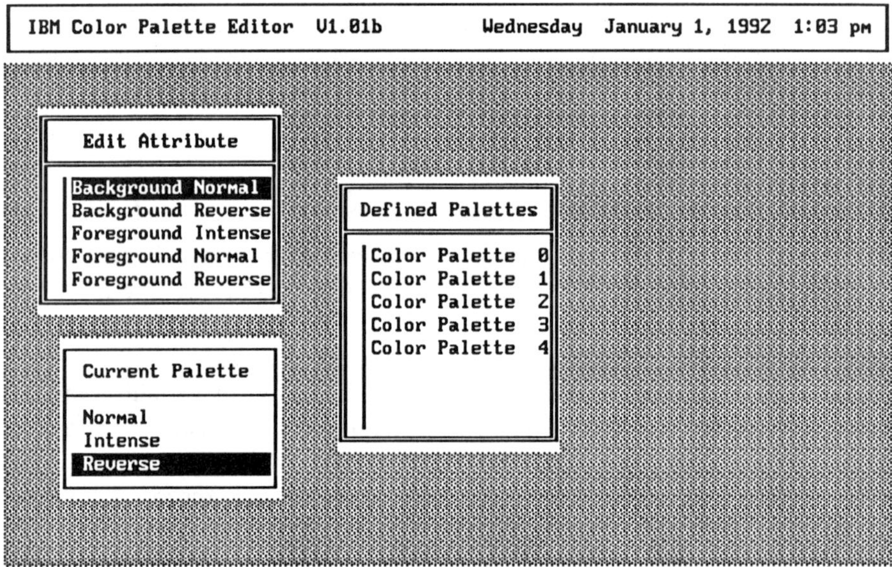

5. Turn to Module 78 to continue the learning sequence.

Module 21
COMCHECK
(ver 2.x and 3.x)

DESCRIPTION

COMCHECK is an installation utility used to test for successful communication between nodes on a Novell network. It attempts to locate and communicate with any other PCs to which it is attached, and it provides a list of those that it finds. COMCHECK is run with the network down. Any nodes to be tested are booted with DOS. Then the appropriate IPX.COM is loaded (Module 8). If the fileserver is to be tested, it too should be booted with DOS and a properly configured IPX. Finally, the COMCHECK program is executed at each node. It is located on an installation diskette. Under *NetWare* 3.1 this is the DOS/DOS ODI WORKSTATION SERVICE diskette; under 2.2 it is on the WSGEN diskette. COMCHECK will prompt you for a station name. Type in anything you please, but each node being tested must have a unique name. COMCHECK will now display a screen showing each node with which it is successfully communicating. The screen is updated periodically.

APPLICATIONS

Use COMCHECK to isolate communication faults on the network. These can be the result of cable breaks or shorts, bad cable connections, defective network interface cards, or defective PCs.

TYPICAL OPERATION

This utility should only be used by knowledgeable network administrators or technicians on a downed network. First boot DOS on the node to be tested. Begin with the boot diskette containing the appropriate IPX inserted and at a DOS prompt.

1. Type **IPX** and press **Enter**. The screen resembles:

```
A:\>IPX
Novell IPX/SPX v3.02 Rev. A (901218)
(C) Copyright 1985, 1990 Novell Inc.  All Rights Reserved.

LAN Option: SEEQ 16 Bit SHELL Driver V2.36EC (910301)
Hardware Configuration: I/O Base = 300h, no ROM, IRQ 11, no DMA

A:\>
```

This display will vary considerably according to the type and configuration of the network interface card being used. Next a diskette with the COMCHECK program should be inserted.

2. Type **COMCHECK** and press **Enter**. You are prompted for a unique name (perhaps the first name of the user that normally works at this workstation).

3. Type a unique name, such as **SUNSHINE**, and press **Enter**.

   Proceed to the other node(s) to be tested and repeat these steps. A typical screen resembles this:

```
NetWare Communication Check  v2.00              Tuesday January  1, 1992  8:27 pm

 Network  Node          Unique User Information        Yr Mo Dy Hr Mn Sc *

 00000001 00801B00350B SUNSHINE                        92/01/01 20:27:39 *
```

4. When you have finished testing, reboot the PCs.

5. Turn to Module 48 to continue the learning sequence.

Module 22
CONFIG
(ver 2.x and 3.x)

DESCRIPTION

CONFIG is a console command which provides information about how the fileserver is configured. CONFIG displays the fileserver's name, the types of NICs installed in the server and how each is configured, and other information. For a more complete discussion of NICs see Module 2. Because of the conceptual differences between *NetWare* 2.x and 3.x, the command will provide different information for each.

Information provided by CONFIG

NetWare 2.x

Fileserver name   Configuration of each Disk Channel
Number of Service Processes   Channel number
Configuration of each NIC   Controller type
     Network address   Interrupt setting
     Lan type (i.e., Ethernet)   I/O Base address
     Interrupt setting
     I/O Base address
     DMA/RAM address

NetWare 3.x

Fileserver name
IPX internal network number
Configuration of each NIC
     Name of LAN driver
     Interrupt setting
     I/O Base address
     Node address
     Frame type
     Board name
     Lan protocol

The interrupt and I/O base address is set on the NIC with switches, or on some boards with software that writes to nonvolatile memory on the board. The LAN driver must be configured to match its corresponding board. The server name is determined at the time of installation with *NetWare* 2.x but can be changed at any time with 3.x. It is usually chosen to be descriptive of the use of that particular server. With the disk controller, the board and drive must also be configured to match. The node address of a server's NICs must be unique from any other NICs on the same network. Remember, each NIC in a fileserver represents a separate network. All nodes on these networks, however, communicate transparently. With 3.x, each NIC can be assigned a unique descriptive board name.

Under *NetWare* 3.x, configuration information is also available using MONITOR (Module 55) either at the fileserver, or from a workstation running RCONSOLE (Module 71).

APPLICATIONS

CONFIG is useful when modifying or expanding a network. By listing the current configuration, you can determine what options are still available for add-on cards. You can also list network addresses which are needed when establishing additional bridges.

TYPICAL OPERATION

In this activity you determine the types of NICs, and their current settings, contained in the fileserver. Begin at the : prompt of your fileserver.

1. Type **CONFIG** and press **Enter.**

```
:CONFIG
File server name: MAIN
IPX internal network number: 00000033

NE-1000 LAN Driver  V3.10 (900608)
     Hardware setting: I/O Port 300h to 31Fh, Interrupt 3h
     Node address: 000009000000
     Frame type: ETHERNET_802.3
     No board name defined
     LAN protocol: IPX network 00000001

Turbo RX-Net LAN Driver  v1.12 (910107)
     Hardware setting: I/O Port 2E0h to 2E8h, Memory D0000h to D3FFFh, Interrupt
  2h
     Node address: 00000000007F
     Frame type: NOVELL_RX-NET
     No board name defined
     LAN protocol: IPX network 00000003
:
```

2. Turn to Module 24 to continue the learning sequence.

Module 23
CONSOLE
(ver 2.x)

DESCRIPTION

With *NetWare* 2.x, fileservers can also be used as workstations. These are referred to as *Nondedicated* fileservers. When a nondedicated server is booted (see Module 8), the server portion of the *NetWare* software is executed, then a DOS shell is loaded to allow you to run DOS applications concurrent to the server's other duties. While in this "workstation mode," CONSOLE commands cannot be executed on the server. The CONSOLE command (usually located on the server's boot diskette) switches back to the "fileserver mode," allowing the use of any console command. The console command DOS (see Module 31) switches the server back to the workstation mode.

APPLICATIONS

Use the CONSOLE command along with the DOS command (see Module 31) to use a nondedicated server alternately as a workstation or a fileserver console. While a nondedicated server is usually left in the workstation mode, there are times when you may wish to execute console commands. This is especially true when bringing down the fileserver. As with any server, the console command DOWN (see Module 32) must be issued prior to turning off a nondedicated server.

NOTE
Nondedicated fileservers have several inherent problems. When in the workstation mode, there is the risk that the user at that workstation might do something to lock up or reset the system. This can down the fileserver causing not only a work interruption for all attached users, but possibly data corruption. Further, a nondedicated fileserver shares its processing power with the workstation's tasks and therefore can cause an overall degradation of network performance for all attached users. It is best to avoid the use of nondedicated fileservers, particularly in medium or large networks or in mission-critical environments.

TYPICAL OPERATION

In this activity you use CONSOLE to switch a nondedicated fileserver to the fileserver mode. Then, issue the console command TIME (Module 88) to display the fileserver's current date and time setting. Begin at the DOS prompt of your nondedicated fileserver.

1. Type **CONSOLE** and press **Enter**. Your screen now displays a : prompt.

2. At the :, type **TIME** and press **Enter**.

3. Turn to Module 31 to continue the learning sequence.

Module 24
DCONFIG
(ver 2.x and 3.x)

DESCRIPTION

DCONFIG provides an easy way to change the configuration of essential program files associated with *NetWare*. The nodes of a Novell network can include fileserver, workstations, and external bridges. Each runs a *NetWare* program that establishes and maintains communication with the other nodes. In each case, the appropriate program is configured by the installer with information concerning the hardware configuration of that node.

In both 2.x and 3.x, workstations use a program called IPX.COM. It is created by a utility called WSGEN (2.x) or SHGEN (3.x), and at the time of creation the installer indicates the type of NIC, the interrupt number, I/O base address, and other information about the current settings on the NIC. Some of this information can be altered after IPX.COM has been generated with DCONFIG. For each type of NIC (i.e., Ethernet, ARCnet, Token Ring), there is a lan driver which is linked into IPX.COM. Each lan driver has several standard configurations. DCONFIG can modify IPX to a different configuration but cannot change the lan driver type.

In 2.x, DCONFIG can also change information embedded in the fileserver program (NET$OS.EXE) and the bridge program (ROUTER.EXE). *NetWare* 3.x is configured dynamically and does not require or allow the use of DCONFIG for this purpose. Once again, the hard disk controller drive type cannot be changed, but rather just the configuration of it. With 2.x, DCONFIG can also change the number of buffers the fileserver supports, another parameter which is dynamically allocated by 3.x. More buffers will use up more of the fileserver's RAM but can provide improved performance.

APPLICATIONS

Use DCONFIG to change parameters about fileserver, workstation, and external bridge hardware. These parameters by nature can conflict with other hardware options installed in PCs, and therefore can require resetting when cards are changed or added. DCONFIG allows you to make such changes without going through the more involved process of regenerating the *NetWare* programs from scratch.

TYPICAL OPERATION

The use of DCONFIG is fairly technical and should only be performed by trained *NetWare* technicians or knowledgeable administrators. See the *NetWare* installation manuals for step-by-step procedures.

Turn to Module 27 to continue the learning sequence.

Module 25
DISABLE LOGIN
(ver 2.x and 3.x)

DESCRIPTION

DISABLE LOGIN is a console command that locks out all workstations from logging in (see Module 48). Workstations already logged in to the fileserver are not affected by the command until they log out. This command is canceled by ENABLE LOGIN (see Module 34).

APPLICATIONS

Before bringing down a fileserver (see Module 32) it is important to have all workstations log out. To facilitate this process, prevent any new workstation from logging in with DISABLE LOGIN. The command can also be useful when troubleshooting problems, especially on large networks. Finally, it can be used to keep users off during system backups or applications updates.

TYPICAL OPERATION

In this activity you prevent all workstations that are currently logged out from logging in to the fileserver. As this command can adversely affect many users, it should only be tried by or with the supervision of a network administrator. Begin at the : prompt of your fileserver.

1. Type **DISABLE LOGIN** and press **Enter**.

Now verify that you cannot log in to the fileserver. This example assumes your username to be FRED with the password SUNSHINE.

2. From a workstation that is not logged in, at a DOS prompt, type **LOGIN** and press **Enter**.

3. Type **FRED** and press **Enter**.

4. Type **SUNSHINE** and press **Enter** when prompted for your password. The screen displays:

```
F:\>LOGIN
Enter your login name: FRED
MAIN/FRED: This account has expired or been disabled by the supervisor.
You are attached to server MAIN.


F:\LOGIN>
```

5. Turn to Module 34 to continue the learning sequence.

Module 26
DISABLE TRANSACTIONS (TTS)
(ver 2.x and 3.x)

DESCRIPTION

NetWare has an advanced system fault tolerant feature called Transactional Tracking System (or TTS). This allows application programmers to package "transactions" together, which are a set of database updates. As an example, when an accounting program produces an invoice, it may make entries to several databases. The customer, inventory, invoice, accounts receivable, and general ledger can all be affected. If the program were interupted in the middle of this process, the various files would lose their integrity. By instructing *NetWare* to treat these updates as a single transaction, it allows *NetWare* to back out that transaction if it is not properly completed. The console command DISABLE TRANSACTIONS (*NetWare* 2.x) or DISABLE TTS (*NetWare* 3.x) has the same effect of temporarily disabling this feature of *NetWare*.

This may sound complicated, but don't worry! It is a command with little application for the typical user.

APPLICATIONS

Use the appropriate form of this command to halt transaction tracking at the fileserver. TTS is resumed by either issuing the ENABLE TRANSACTIONS/ENABLE TTS command, or when the fileserver is downed and brought back up. This is typically only used by programmers wishing to troubleshoot software.

TYPICAL OPERATION

In this activity you disable transaction tracking on a *NetWare* 2.x fileserver. Begin at the : at the fileserver.

1. Type **DISABLE TRANSACTIONS** and press **Enter**.
2. Turn to Module 35 to continue the learning sequence.

Module 27
DISK
(ver 2.x)

DESCRIPTION

The console command DISK is only valid in *NetWare* versions 2.x. *NetWare* 3.x can obtain similar information with the MONITOR NLM (Module 55) either at the fileserver or at a workstation running RCONSOLE (Module 71). DISK displays various information concerning the hard disks on your network. The display is similar to the following:

```
PHYSICAL DISK STATUS AND STATISTICS
          cha     con     drv     stat    IO Err  Free    Used
    00    1       0       0       OK      5       495     5
```

Following the drive number you see the channel and controller number to which the drive is attached. Also reported is the drive's status: "OK" (no problems), "NO HOT" (hot fix is not running on this drive), or "OFF" (this drive is shut down). (*Hot Fix* detects bad disk blocks and redirects data destined for the bad areas to a reserve of disk blocks established by *NetWare* for that purpose.) DISK also shows the total number of disk errors detected since installation, the number of blocks available for redirected data, and the number so far in use. The drive status will continue to be monitored until you issue the OFF command (see Module 62).

APPLICATIONS

As a network grows, there is often a need to add new network drives. In planning such expansion, DISK provides important information about existing drives and how they are physically attached. Also DISK allows the network administrator to monitor the performance of network drives, locate defective drives, and possibly discover drives with excessive errors that are on the verge of complete failure.

TYPICAL OPERATION

In this activity you display the status of network drives. Begin at the : prompt of your fileserver.

1. Type **DISK** and press **Enter**. You see the "Physical Status and Statistics" display.
2. To clear the DISK screen, type **OFF** and press **Enter**.
3. Turn to Module 56 to continue the learning sequence.

Module 28
DISMOUNT
(ver 2.x and 3.x)

DESCRIPTION

The console command DISMOUNT is used to inform *NetWare* to no longer service a volume. A volume is a partition on a fileserver drive. The entire capacity of a drive can be allocated one volume or it can be divided into several. Under *NetWare* 3.x, a volume can span more than one drive.

Under *NetWare* 2.x, this command is only used with fileservers that use removable media as a shared device. DISMOUNT writes any cached data (that which is being held in RAM) to the removable volume and closes any open files. If the removable volume is a pack of diskettes, use the DISMOUNT PACK version of the command. With either version, follow the command with the appropriate volume number. Nonremovable volumes are automatically mounted when the fileserver is booted, and dismounted when the fileserver is downed (Module 32).

With 3.x versions, *NetWare* must be told to mount and dismount volumes, even if they are nonremovable. This can be done with manually typed commands, but typically volumes are mounted by the AUTOEXEC.NCF file (see Module 8) and dismounted by the DOWN command.

APPLICATIONS

NetWare holds certain disk information in RAM memory. When changing removable media or replacing a hard drive, *NetWare* must be informed so that this cached information is written to disk, and the volume is no longer accessible to users. Use DISMOUNT and MOUNT (see modules 28 and 56) to keep *NetWare* informed of such changes.

TYPICAL OPERATION

In this activity you prepare to remove a volume from use by telling *NetWare* to "shut down" the volume. This exercise should only be performed by or with the assistance of a knowledgeable network administrator. Begin at the : prompt of your fileserver.

1. Type **DISMOUNT 1** and press **Enter**.
2. Turn to Module 46 to continue the learning sequence.

Module 29
DISPLAY NETWORKS
(ver 2.x and 3.x)

DESCRIPTION

The console command DISPLAY NETWORKS lists all attached networks with which the fileserver is in communication. This includes the network attached to each fileserver NIC, the internal IPX network that each Novell fileserver has, and any networks attached via external bridges or routers. Three things are displayed for each network: the network address, the number of hops that separate the network from the fileserver, and the length of time that it should take a packet of data to reach from the fileserver to that network (in eighths of a second).

APPLICATIONS

Use DISPLAY NETWORKS to determine what networks have access to a fileserver and how quickly information stored on that fileserver can be transferred to those networks.

TYPICAL OPERATION

In this activity you display a list of the networks with which your fileserver is in communication. Start at the : prompt of the fileserver.

1. Type **DISPLAY NETWORKS** and press **Enter**.
2. Turn to Module 32 to continue the learning sequence.

Module 30
DISPLAY SERVERS
(ver 2.x and 3.x)

DESCRIPTION

The console command DISPLAY SERVERS lists all other fileservers with which a given fileserver is in communication. This command is only useful on networks with more than one fileserver. This information is also available at a workstation via the SLIST command (Module 84). In addition to the name of each fileserver, DISPLAY SERVERS lists the number of hops data must make in order to reach that server.

APPLICATIONS

Use DISPLAY SERVERS to determine what fileservers are linked to a given server.

TYPICAL OPERATION

In this activity you display a list of the fileservers with which your fileserver is in communication. Start at the : prompt of the fileserver.

1. Type **DISPLAY FILESERVERS** and press **Enter**.
2. Turn to Module 29 to continue the learning sequence.

Module 31
DOS
(ver 2.x)

DESCRIPTION

The console command DOS is used on nondedicated fileservers to switch from the "fileserver mode" to the "workstation mode." After you issue the DOS command (or after it is automatically issued by the boot diskette), applications can be run on the server as though it were a workstation. This only applies to *NetWare* 2.x, as 3.x does not support the use of nondedicated fileservers. For a more complete explanation of this process, see Module 23.

APPLICATIONS

Use the DOS command, along with the CONSOLE command, to use a nondedicated fileserver alternately as a workstation or a fileserver console.

TYPICAL OPERATION

In this activity you return a nondedicated fileserver to the workstation mode. Begin at the : prompt of your nondedicated fileserver. (You changed to fileserver mode in Module 23.)

1. Type **DOS** and press **Enter**. Your screen now returns to a DOS prompt.

2. Turn to Module 72 to continue the learning sequence.

Module 32
DOWN
(ver 2.x and 3.x)

DESCRIPTION

The console command DOWN prepares a fileserver to be powered off. This is the final step in "bringing down" a fileserver (see Module 8). *NetWare* allocates a portion of RAM memory to caching (or buffering) hard disks. This process speeds overall system performance, but it means that at any given moment crucial information may be held in RAM and not recorded to the hard disk. If the server is powered down in such a state, data can be lost or corrupted. The DOWN command tells *NetWare* to record all such information to disk. All workstations should be logged out of the fileserver (or at least have no active files) before you issue the DOWN command.

APPLICATIONS

Always issue the DOWN command at a fileserver console before powering down the fileserver!

TYPICAL OPERATION

In this activity you prepare a fileserver to be powered down. Begin at the : prompt of your fileserver. Before trying this exercise, be sure that all workstations are logged out (see Module 49).

   1. Type **DOWN** and press **Enter**. The screen displays:

```
:DOWN
MAIN has been shut down. Please Re-Boot to Restart.

:
```

If there are workstations that are still logged in to the fileserver, the screen displays:

```
: DOWN

WARNING


ACTIVE FILES OPEN, HALT NETWORK?
```

2. Type **N** to halt the DOWNing of the network. Log out the workstation(s) or use CLEAR STATION (see Module 23). Now repeat step 1.

   Congratulations! You have completed the learning sequence.

Module 33
EDIT
(ver 3.x)

DESCRIPTION

EDIT is a *NetWare* Loadable Module (NLM) that permits you to edit small text files located on the fileserver. It is most frequently used to edit the AUTOEXEC.NCF file.

APPLICATIONS

To make modifications to the AUTOEXEC.NCF file (or any small text file located on the fileserver), use EDIT. This can also be done via INSTALL NLM (see Module 46).

TYPICAL OPERATION

In this activity you view the contents of the AUTOEXEC.NCF file. Start at the : prompt of a 3.x fileserver.

1. Type **LOAD EDIT** and press **Enter**.
2. Type **SYS:SYSTEM\ AUTOEXEC.NCF** and press **Enter**.

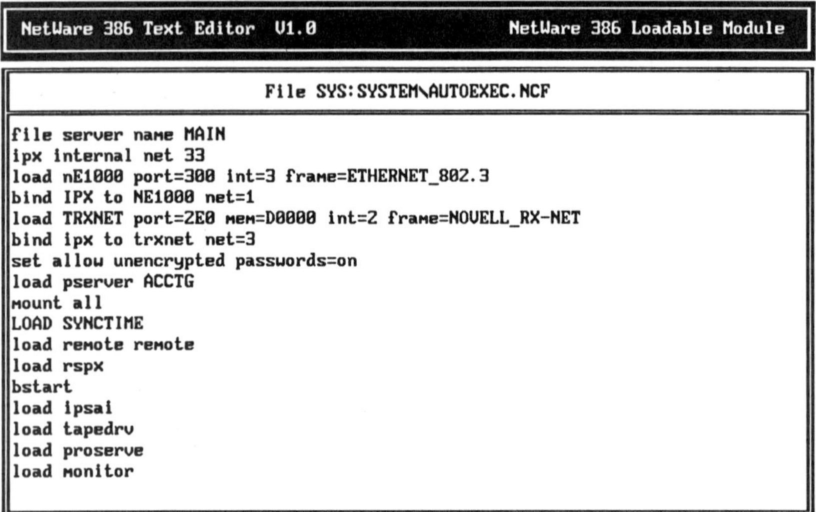

3. When finished, exit EDIT via the **Esc** key.
4. Turn to Module 53 to continue the learning sequence.

Module 34
ENABLE LOGIN
(ver 2.x and 3.x)

DESCRIPTION

ENABLE LOGIN is a console command that negates the effect of DISABLE LOGIN (see Module 25). It restores the ability for workstations to log in (see Module 48) to the fileserver.

APPLICATIONS

After completing a task for which DISABLE LOGIN was issued, use ENABLE LOGIN to restore the server to its normal status.

TYPICAL OPERATION

In this activity, you reenable the ability to log in to a fileserver. You DISABLEd LOGIN in Module 25. Begin at the : prompt of your fileserver.

1. Type **ENABLE LOGIN** and press **Enter**.

Now verify that workstations can log in. This example assumes your username to be FRED and your password, SUNSHINE.

2. From a workstation that is not logged in, type **LOGIN FRED** and press **Enter**.

3. Type **SUNSHINE** and press **Enter** when prompted for a password. You are now logged in as usual.

4. Turn to Module 19 to continue the learning sequence.

Module 35
ENABLE TRANSACTIONS (TTS)
(ver 2.x and 3.x)

DESCRIPTION

NetWare has an advanced system fault tolerant feature called Transactional Tracking System (or TTS). This allows application programmers to package "transactions" together, which are a set of database updates. For a more detailed explanation of this process, see DISABLE TRANSACTIONS (Module 26). The console command DISABLE TRANSACTIONS has the effect of temporarily disabling this feature of *NetWare*. ENABLE TRANSACTIONS (for *NetWare* 2.x) or ENABLE TTS (for *NetWare* 3.x) reenables the TTS system.

This may sound complicated, but don't worry! It is a command with little application for the typical user.

APPLICATIONS

Use the appropriate form of this command to reenable transaction tracking at the fileserver.

TYPICAL OPERATION

In this activity you reenable transaction tracking on a *NetWare* 2.x fileserver. Begin at the : at the fileserver.

1. Type **ENABLE TRANSACTIONS** and press **Enter**.
2. Turn to Module 30 to continue the learning sequence.

Module 36
ENDCAP
(ver 2.x and 3.x)

DESCRIPTION

ENDCAP is a public command which closes printer spool files opened with the CAPTURE command (see Module 14). These spooled files are then sent to the appropriate print queues. ENDCAP redirects subsequent printer output back to your workstation's local printer port(s).

ENDCAP need not always be issued manually. *NetWare* issues an automatic ENDCAP with each CAPTURE, NPRINT, LOGIN, and LOGOUT command. Under DOS 3.0 and above, ENDCAP is automatically issued each time you exit an application. This automatic feature can be disabled using the NoAutoendcap flag with the CAPTURE command (see Module 14). ENDCAPs are also issued automatically at specific intervals following output while you are in an application if you use the TI flag with the CAPTURE command.

There are five optional flags. You may use the full name or the abbreviation.

ALL	This flag causes ENDCAP to release all local printer ports. This is the default.
C (Cancel)	This flag causes ENDCAP to release LPT1: and delete any CAPTUREd print jobs without sending them to a print queue.
CALL (Cancel ALL)	This flag has the same effect as the Cancel flag, except that it affects all local printer ports.
CL= (CancelLocal=)	The parameter immediately following CL is a valid local printer port number (0-2). This flag has the same effect as the Cancel flag, except that it affects only the local printer port specified.
L= (Local=)	The parameter immediately following L is a valid local printer port number (0-2). This flag cancels the CAPTURE of the specified local printer port, sending spooled output to the appropriate print queue.

APPLICATIONS

Use ENDCAP in conjunction with CAPTURE (see Module 14) to direct printer output to network printers.

TYPICAL OPERATION

In this activity you close any CAPTUREd files from LPT1 and send them to the appropriate network printers. Begin at the DOS prompt of a logged-in workstation.

1. Type **ENDCAP** and press **Enter**. Notice the display:

```
F:\>ENDCAP
Device LPT1: set to local mode.

F:\>
```

2. Turn to Module 60 to continue the learning sequence.

Module 37
FCONSOLE
(ver 2.x and 3.x)

DESCRIPTION

FCONSOLE is a menu-driven utility that allows you to view certain information and perform certain tasks relating to the fileserver. Some of the options are limited to users with supervisor equivalency or users that have been designated as console operators. Supervisors and console operators are created under SYSCON (Module 86). *NetWare* 3.x has a utility called RCONSOLE (Module 71) that allows you to "capture" the fileserver console from a workstation and issue all console commands. Therefore, FCONSOLE is most useful on 2.x networks. Further, several of the options in FCONSOLE are not supported under *NetWare* 3.x. If you select one of these, FCONSOLE simply displays a message stating that the feature is not supported under your version of *NetWare*.

The main menu options of FCONSOLE are:

Broadcast Console Message	This has the same effect as the console command BROADCAST (Module 13). Messages are sent to all workstations and fileservers. This selection requires supervisor privileges.
Change Current Fileserver	This allows you to select which fileserver is your current default and log in to or log out of the fileserver. Obviously, this is not used on networks with only one fileserver.
Connection Information	This provides a list of everyone currently connected (logged in or attached) to the fileserver. If you have supervisor privileges, you can select any of these connections and view a submenu. Through the submenu you can view various information about that connection, send a message to the user at that connection, or disconnect that user from the fileserver.
Down Fileserver	This selection has the same effect as the console command DOWN (Module 32). Through FCONSOLE, however, you can do this from any workstation. Obviously, this requires supervisor privileges.

File/Lock Activity (*NetWare* 2.x only)	This allows you to view current information about the status of files, particularly in regards to locks placed on them. This is rather technical information and is most useful to programmers. It is only available to users with supervisor privileges.
LAN Driver Information (*NetWare* 2.x only)	This displays information about the network interface card(s) installed in the fileserver. This includes NIC type, address, node, and interrupt.
Purge All Salvageable Files (*NetWare* 2.x only)	This selection has the same effect as the public command PURGE (Module 71). It ensures that any recently erased files cannot be SALVAGEd (Module 77). This requires supervisor privileges.
Statistics (*NetWare* 2.x only)	This provides a wide range of data concerning the operation of the network. Information it gives on disk usage, memory allocations, and much more can be useful to a network engineer in establishing the most efficient configuration of the network. This, too, is reserved for users with supervisor privileges.
Status	This lists fileserver date and time, tells you if LOGIN has been disabled and tells if Transaction Tracking System is active.
Version	This displays the version of *NetWare* currently running on the fileserver.

APPLICATIONS

FCONSOLE combines a few features that are of use to everyone with many advanced features that are of interest to supervisors, administrators, programmers, and other technically-oriented individuals. The features that are useful to all users can be duplicated with individual commands, so FCONSOLE is of greatest use to the latter group mentioned above. The technical information provided by this utility can allow a great deal of insight as to the degree of efficiency of the network. This is important both in determining the ideal configuration of newer networks and in planning expansion of established networks.

TYPICAL OPERATION

In this activity you use one of the FCONSOLE selections that is available to all users to display the type of network interface card (and related information) that is in your fileserver. Begin at the DOS prompt of a logged-in workstation.

1. Type **FCONSOLE** and press **Enter**. Your screen resembles this:

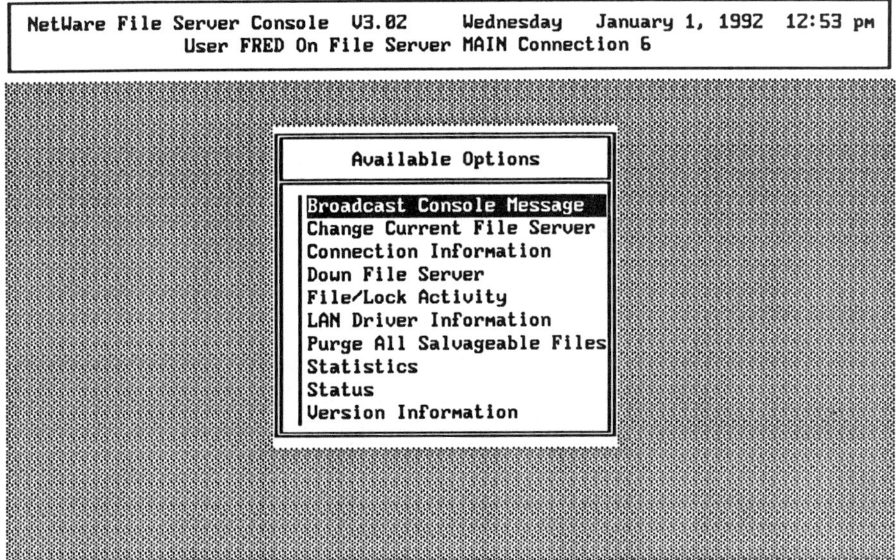

2. Press **Down Arrow** to highlight LAN Driver Information, then press **Enter**. The screen resembles the following:

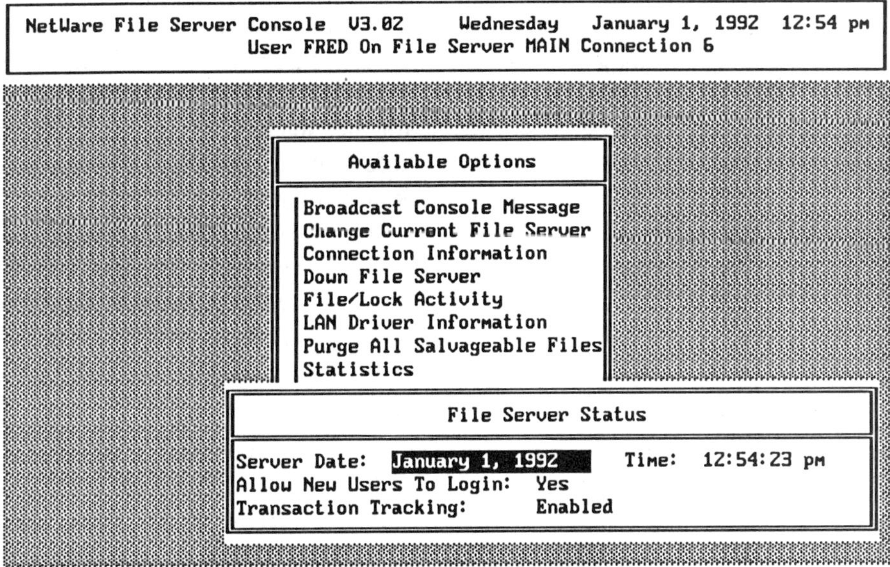

3. Exit FCONSOLE by pressing **Esc** twice, then press **Enter**.
4. Turn to Module 55 to continue the learning sequence.

Module 38
FILER
(ver 2.x and 3.x)

DESCRIPTION

FILER is a menu-driven utility used to manage network files and directories. Most of the options available through FILER can also be accomplished with public and/or DOS commands. Because FILER is menu-driven, many users will find it to be an easier environment in which to work. While FILER is available to all users, they are restricted from file access according to established rights and trustee assignments. Under *NetWare* 3.x, filer has certain features not found in 2.x. Also, 3.x's use of different file attributes and file rights is reflected in the FILER programs. For a more thorough discussion on *NetWare* file attributes, see FLAG (Module 39); for more on file rights, see GRANT and RIGHTS (modules 41 and 76, respectively). FILER presents the following options:

Current Directory Information	This selection allows you to view a variety of information about the current directory. The current directory is whichever directory you were in when FILER was invoked, or the last directory selected with the Select Current Directory option below. Available information includes creation date, maximum rights mask, and a list of owners and trustees. The owner is the user who created the directory, but can be overwritten with any valid username. Trustees (users who have been assigned privileges to this directory) can be added or deleted using the Insert and Delete keys. You can also list directory attributes (see FLAGDIR, Module 40).
Directory Contents	This selection displays all files and subdirectories in the current directory. You can select a given item using the Arrow keys and Enter. FILER displays information about the selected item, including attributes (e.g., READ ONLY), creation date, last accessed date, last archived date, last modified date, the owner of the file, and the size of the file in bytes. Any of this information can be changed (assuming you have the rights) except the size of file.

Files can be copied to new locations on the network. You need READ and FILE SCAN rights to the source file, and CREATE, MODIFY, and WRITE rights to the target directory. Directories can also be copied. You can copy just the files in a given directory, or the entire directory structure, including all files and subdirectories. When copying multiple items, use the <F5> function key to mark them. Highlight each item to be copied, and press <F5>. That item will begin flashing and remain highlighted after you move the cursor. You cannot mark both files and directories in the same batch operation. When all desired items have been marked, press Enter. You are now presented the following options:

FILE OPTIONS

COPY MARKED FILES
SET ATTRIBUTES
SET CREATION DATE
SET INHERITED RIGHTS
SET LAST ACCESSED DATE
SET LAST MODIFIED DATE
SET OWNER

SUBDIRECTORY OPTIONS

COPY SUBDIRECTORIES FILES
COPY SUBDIRECTORIES STRUCTURE
SET CREATION DATE
SET INHERITED RIGHTS
SET OWNER

Remember, whichever option you select affects all of the items you have marked.

You can delete any item(s) from the list. Select a file with the Arrow keys, then press the Del key. You must, of course, have deletion rights to that item. If you select a subdirectory, you can choose to delete only the files that it contains, or the entire structure, including all files and subdirectories within it. Finally, you can create new subdirectories via the Ins key.

Select Current Directory

This selection lets you select a different directory in which to work. The selection of a new current directory does not affect you when you exit FILER. In other words, the directory from

	which you enter FILER will always be the same as when you leave.
Set Filer Options	This selection has 8 suboptions:
Confirm Deletions	This requires you to confirm that a selected file is to be deleted. The default is to confirm.
Confirm File Copies	This confirms each copy individually.
Confirm File Overwrites	This prevents you from accidentally copying a file to a new directory where another file with the same name already exists. In this event FILER will warn you before the copy takes place.
Directories Exclude Pattern	This lets you specify which directories will not be included when listing directories elsewhere in FILER. On drives with a large number of directories, this can simplify your work. As you may specify multiple patterns, use the Insert and Delete keys to add or remove each pattern. Patterns may include the DOS wild cards "*" and "?" (for example, the pattern A*.* will exclude all directories beginning with the letter A).
Directories Include Pattern	This is exactly like the Directories Exclude Pattern option, except that specified directories will be included in the listings.
File Exclude Pattern	This has the same effect on files as the Directories Exclude Patterns has on directories.
File Include Pattern	This has the same effect on files as the Directories Include Pattern has on directories.
File Search Attributes	This allows you to include SYSTEM and HIDDEN files in the list. Use the Insert and Delete keys to modify.
Directory Search Attributes	This allows you to include SYSTEM and HIDDEN directories in the list.
Volume Information	This selection displays information about the current volume including server name, volume name, volume type, total volume size (in bytes), available bytes, total number of directory entries allowed, and number of entries still available. The total entries available is of interest under *NetWare* 2.x, as this number is preset when the server is installed or modified. If this number is getting low, an administrator or network technician needs to schedule fileserver downtime so that the

total number of entries allowed can be increased. *NetWare* 3.x allocates this value dynamically, so this isn't a problem.

None of this VOLUME information can be changed from within FILER.

APPLICATIONS

FILER provides a comprehensive interface between the user and file/directory related activities. Many users (especially novices) will find the FILER environment easy to understand and use. More experienced users may find the command equivalents of the FILER options to be quicker to invoke.

TYPICAL OPERATION

In this activity you use FILER to change to the directory SYS:INN, create a subdirectory named PRACTICE, and copy the file TEST.TXT into the new subdirectory. Begin at the DOS prompt of a logged-in workstation.

1. Type **FILER** and press **Enter**. Your screen resembles the following:

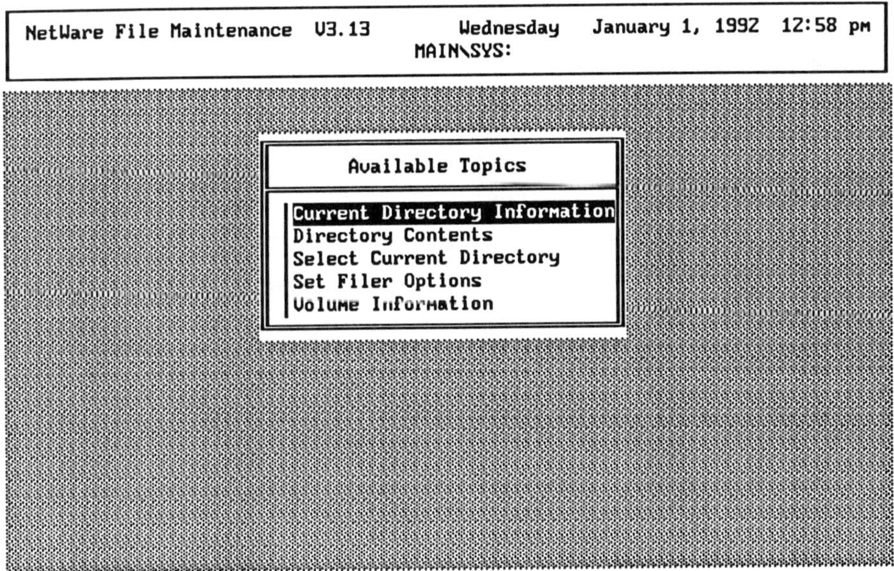

2. Press **Down Arrow** to highlight the third selection, Select Current Directory. Press **Enter**.

3. Press **Backspace** to delete the existing directory name, and type **SYS:INN** in its place. Press **Enter**.

4. Highlight Directory Contents and press **Enter**. The contents of SYS:INN are displayed.

5. Create a new subdirectory by pressing **Ins**. At this point your screen resembles this:

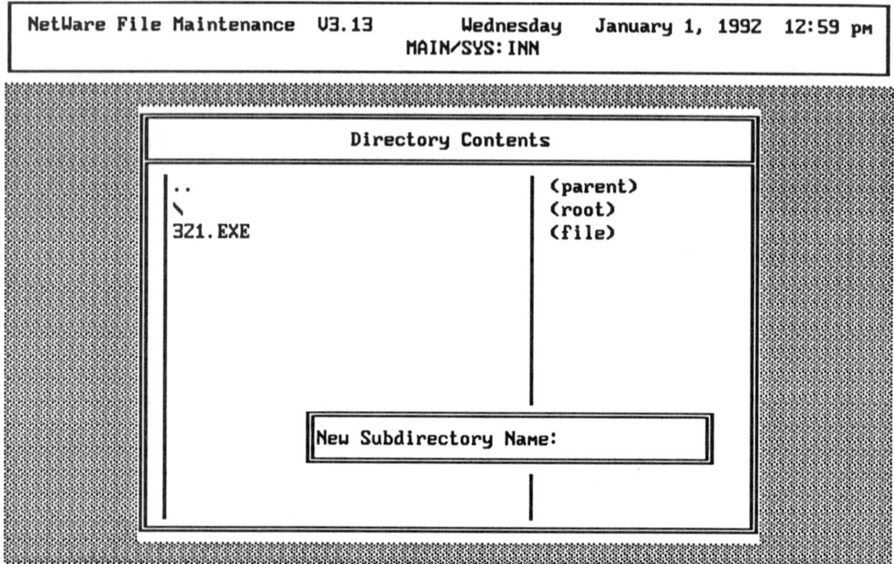

6. Type the new subdirectory name, **PRACTICE**, and press **Enter**. It now appears in the list.

7. Press **Esc** to return to the listing of directory contents.

8. Highlight the file named TEST.TXT and press **Enter**. Your screen shows:

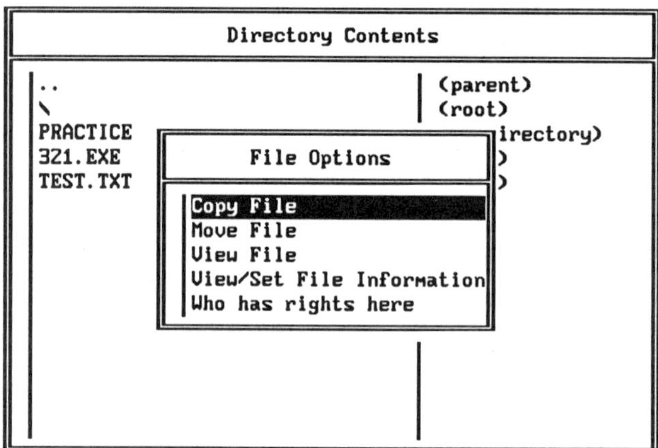

9. Highlight Copy File and press **Enter**.

You are now prompted for the name of the destination directory. Use the subdirectory you just created; you must precede it with its full path name. The name of the fileserver may be omitted; *NetWare* will fill it in with the current default.

10. Type **SYS:INN\PRACTICE** and press **Enter**. At this point the screen resembles the following:

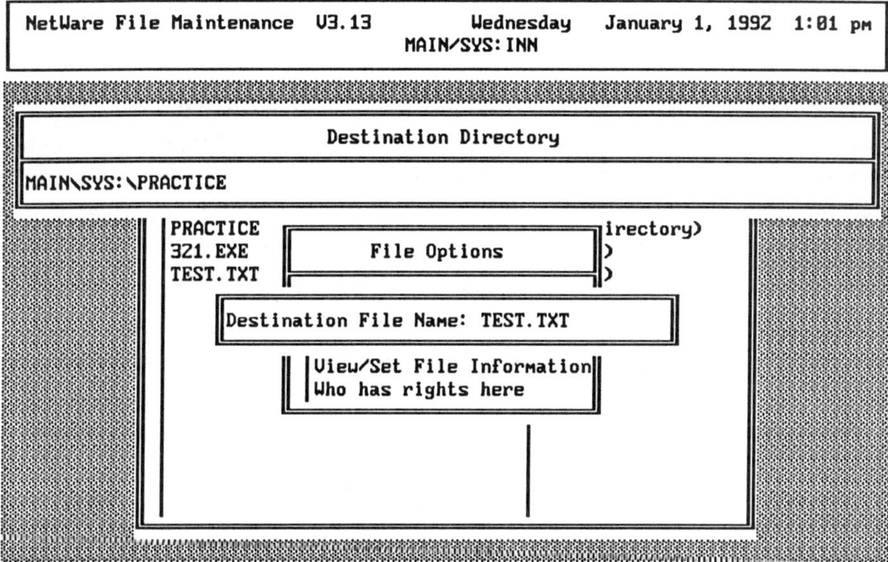

11. The name TEST.TXT is fine, so press **Enter**.

12. Press **Alt-F10** and press **Enter** to exit FILER.

13. Turn to Module 33 to continue the learning sequence.

Module 39
FLAG
(ver 2.x and 3.x)

DESCRIPTION

FLAG is a public command used to display and/or change the attributes of specified files. The command can be followed by a complete path and filename and can include the DOS wild cards "*" or "?". If you do not specify a path or filename, all files in the current default directory are assumed. Unlike most *NetWare* commands, FLAG requires the use of at least one flag to cause a change. If you use the command alone, *NetWare* simply lists the current attributes of the designated files.

Each flag may be preceded with "+" or "-" to add or delete that attribute respectively. When adding and deleting in the same command, all additions must be grouped together, as must all deletions. By omitting the "+" or "-", *NetWare* assumes you want to add that attribute. If the attribute already exists for this file, the command will have no effect.

Please note that the attribute set for *NetWare* 3.x differs from that for *NetWare* 2.x. The following flags are used with the FLAG command. You can use the full name or the abbreviation of the flag.

FLAG options for both 2.x and 3.x:

C (Continuous)	This flag causes the information reported by FLAG to scroll continuously on your screen. Otherwise, you must press a key to continue after every screenfull.
H (Hidden)	Hides files. When users scan the files in a directory using the DOS DIR command, hidden files will not be listed. Hidden files can also not be erased or copied. This command has the same effect as HIDEFILE (Module 43). To make a file visible again, use "-H", which has the same effect as SHOWFILE (Module 83).
N (Normal)	Denotes the default file attributes. These are -S and -RO or Non-shareable and Read/Write.
RA (Read Audit)	This flag has no assigned use at present.

RO (Read Only)	Prohibits users from writing to this file. The file cannot be modified, deleted, or renamed. The negative value of this flag (-RO) is also known as "read/write" and is the default for newly created files.
S (Shareable)	Allows concurrent access to a file by multiple users. It is typically used on the program and data files of "networkable" or "multiuser" applications.
SUB (Subdirectory)	This flag will cause the FLAG command to affect not only files in the current directory, but also in any subdirectories.
SY (System)	Marks files as being "system." This has the same effect as Hidden.
T (Transactional)	Protects the integrity of a file by protecting it with TTS (transactional tracking system). This is a system fault tolerence (SFT) feature that ensures that partial changes to files are not permitted, as in the case where a system loses power in the middle of a database update. See TTS (Module 35).
WA (Write Audit)	This flag has no assigned use at present.

Flag options for 2.x only:

A (All)	Assigns all file attributes supported under your current version of *NetWare*.
I (Indexed)	Invokes "turbo FAT indexing." This provides a very rapid lookup table for the location of large files, providing faster access to their data. At the time of *NetWare* installation, the maximum number of indexed files is set.

Flag options for 3.x only:

ALL (All)	Assigns all file attributes supported under your current version of *NetWare*.
A (Archive Needed)	Marks a file as needing to be backed up. Normally *NetWare*, just like DOS, will mark a file as Archive Needed when any change is made to that file. After the file is archived (or backed up), the Archive Needed flag is removed until further changes warrant. This flag allows you to manually mark (or unmark) files in this regard.
X (Execute Only)	This flag is unique in that it can only be invoked by a supervisor equivalent, and it has no negative value—that is it cannot be removed. It is used on files with the .COM or .EXE extension (executable program files). Once assigned, the file

cannot be copied. It is useful in assuring adherence to copyright laws. It also will ensure that users don't copy program files into their own directories. Without this, an administrator could revoke a user's rights to a given application, and yet the user could still access a previously made copy.

CI (Copy Inhibit)	This flag will prohibit users from copying a file. It will only work with Macintosh files.
DI (Delete Inhibit)	This flag prevents users from deleting a file. NOTE: If this flag is used but a user has the right to modify this file, they can simply issue the -DI flag and then delete it!
RI (Rename Inhibit)	This flag prevents users from renaming a file. NOTE: If this flag is used but a user has the right to modify this file, they can simply issue the -RI flag and then rename it!

TYPICAL OPERATION

In this activity you display the attributes of all files in the default directory, then set them all to the Read/Write Non-shareable status. Begin at the DOS prompt of a logged-in workstation.

1. Type **FLAG** and press **Enter**. Your screen resembles this:

```
F:\>FLAG
     AUTOEXEC.BAT  [ Rw - A - - -- - - -- -- - - - ]
     CONFIG.SYS    [ Rw - A - - -- - - -- -- - - - ]
     IBMDOS.COM    [ Ro - - - H Sy - - -- -- - D R ]
     BACKOUT.TTS   [ Rw - A - H Sy - - -- -- - - - ]
     DMSZ30.CFG    [ Rw - A - - -- - - -- -- - - - ]
     DMSZ30.ERR    [ Rw - - - -- - - -- -- - - - ]
     IBMBIO.COM    [ Ro - - - H Sy - - -- -- - D R ]
     EDIT.COM      [ Rw - A - - -- - - -- -- - - - ]
```

2. Type **FLAG *.* N** and press **Enter**. Notice the display:

```
F:\>FLAG *.* N
     AUTOEXEC.BAT  [ Rw - A - - -- - - -- -- - - - ]
     CONFIG.SYS    [ Rw - A - - -- - - -- -- - - - ]
     IBMDOS.COM    [ Rw - - - - -- - - -- -- - - - ]
File in use
     BACKOUT.TTS   [ Rw - A - - -- - - -- -- - - - ]
     DMSZ30.CFG    [ Rw - A - - -- - - -- -- - - - ]
     DMSZ30.ERR    [ Rw - - - -- - - -- -- - - - ]
     IBMBIO.COM    [ Rw - - - -- - - -- -- - - - ]
     EDIT.COM      [ Rw - A - - -- - - -- -- - - - ]
```

3. Turn to Module 40 to continue the learning sequence.

Module 40
FLAGDIR
(ver 2.x and 3.x)

DESCRIPTION

FLAGDIR is a public command used to display and/or change the attributes of specified directories. The command can be followed by a complete path and directory name and can include the DOS wild cards "*" or "?". If you do not specify a path or directory name, all directories in the current default directory are assumed. Each flag may be preceded with "+" or "-" to add or delete that attribute respectively. When adding and deleting in the same command, all additions must be grouped together, as must all deletions. By omitting the "+" or "-", *NetWare* assumes you want to add that attribute. If the attribute already exists for this directory, the command will have no effect.

Please note that the attribute set for *NetWare* 3.x differs from that for *NetWare* 2.x. The following flags are used with the FLAGDIR command. You can use the full name or the abbreviation of the flag.

FLAGDIR options for both 2.x and 3.x:

C (Continuous)   This flag causes the information reported by FLAG to scroll continuously on your screen. Otherwise, you must press a key to continue after every screenfull.

H (Hidden)   Hides directories. When users scan the files in a directory using the DOS DIR command, hidden directories will not be listed. Also, hidden directories cannot be erased or copied. Even though a directory has been hidden, a user can still scan and access the contents of that directory as long, of course, as they have the appropriate rights.

N (Normal)   This flag cancels any attributes that have been set for the specified directories. When a directory is first created, it has no attributes.

SY (System)   This flag marks directories as being crucial to the "system." This has the same effect as Hidden.

Flag options for 2.x only:

PR (Private)
: This flag causes a directory to show up in a DOS DIR scan, but not the directory's contents.

Flag options for 3.x only:

D (Delete Inhibit)
: This flag prevents users from deleting a directory.

P (Purge)
: This flag tells *NetWare* to immediately purge any files within this directory as soon as they are deleted. Thus, SALVAGE (Module 77) has no effect in directories with this attribute.

R (Rename Inhibit)
: This flag prevents users from renaming a file.

TYPICAL OPERATION

In this activity you set the attributes of a directory named \INN to Hidden, then back to Normal. Begin at the DOS prompt of a logged-in workstation.

1. Type **FLAGDIR \INN H** and press **Enter**. Your screen resembles this:

```
F:\>FLAGDIR \INN H
MAIN/SYS:
     INN              Hidden

F:\>
```

2. Type **DIR INN** and press **Enter**. The \INN directory does not appear in the directory listing.

3. Type **FLAGDIR \INN N** and press **Enter**. Notice the display:

```
F:\>FLAGDIR \INN N
MAIN/SYS:
     INN              Normal

F:\>
```

4. Turn to Module 59 to continue the learning sequence.

Module 41
GRANT
(ver 2.x and 3.x)

DESCRIPTION

GRANT is used to assign and delete rights for a given directory. Under *NetWare* 3.x, you can also assign and delete rights for specific files. You must specify a single user or group, as well as the rights you wish to grant (or deny). You also need to specify the directory if it is not the current default. This can be accomplished in a menu-driven environment using SYSCON (see Module 86) or FILER (Module 38). Once you have GRANTed rights to a user for a directory (or file), that user is considered a *trustee*. You can only GRANT rights to directories in which you have ACCESS CONTROL rights. There are eight basic rights available under both versions of *NetWare*, plus one (SUPERVISORY) available only to *NetWare* 3.x. When GRANTing these rights, use the flags listed below.

Flag	Right	Description
R	READ	Open file and read contents.
W	WRITE	Open file and write to it.
C	CREATE	Create new files and directories.
E	ERASE	Delete files and directories.
M	MODIFY	Change file or directory name or attributes.
F	FILE SCAN	See files (but not necessarily open them).
A	ACCESS CONTROL	Grant file or directory rights to other users.
S	SUPERVISORY	Under 3.x, this grants all rights, and overrides any other restrictions that have been placed on this user within this directory structure.
ALL		Grant all eight (or nine) rights.
NR	(NO RIGHTS)	Revoke all rights.

You can display your rights to a directory using the RIGHTS command (see Module 76). A trustee of a directory can be removed using REMOVE (see Module 73).

Follow the GRANT command by the flags that represent the right which is to be changed, the directory (or with 3.x, the filename), and the username in the following manner:

```
GRANT XXX FOR directory name TO username
```

Precede the flags of listed rights by "only" to clear any prexisting rights. You can also use "all but" to GRANT all rights other than those specified.

APPLICATIONS

Use GRANT to quickly and easily allow a user or group to access a given directory. A network administrator can do this to provide access to newly created directories whose contents are of interest to the specified user or group. Users may want to share with others the contents of a directory to which the administrator has given them parental rights. While this can be done with the SYSCON menu utility, experienced users will find GRANT faster.

TYPICAL OPERATION

In this activity you GRANT the user "GUEST" READ and FILE SCAN rights to the SYS:INN directory (as created in Module 8). GUEST is a username which *NetWare* automatically creates during installation. After each of these exercises you can verify that the command has had the desired effect by logging in as GUEST and using the RIGHTS command (see Module 76). Begin at the DOS prompt of a logged-in workstation.

1. Type **GRANT R F FOR SYS:INN TO GUEST** and press **Enter**. Now remove these rights and GRANT only the right to do FILE SCANS of this directory.
2. Type **GRANT ONLY F FOR SYS:INN TO GUEST** and press **Enter**. Finally, GRANT all rights for this directory except Erase.
3. Type **GRANT ALL BUT E FOR SYS:INN TO GUEST** and press **Enter**.
4. Turn to Module 89 to continue the learning sequence.

Module 42
HELP
(ver 2.x and 3.x)

DESCRIPTION

HELP is a menu-driven utility which provides information about the use of other *NetWare* commands and utilities. It is designed to be self-explanatory. The type of menuing system differs from other *NetWare* utilities. HELP uses a pull-down menu system, not unlike many of the popular applications being published today. If your workstation is equipped with a mouse, the menus can be controlled using it. Otherwise, access menus by holding down the Alt key and pressing the first letter of the menu name. For example, from the main help screen, to access the file menu, type Alt-F. Use the arrows and the Enter key to make a selection. Back out of a menu with the Esc key.

There is a quicker way to use HELP if you are looking for help on a specfic *NetWare* command or utility. Simply follow the HELP command with the name of that item. HELP takes you straight to the pertinent information.

To exit HELP, go to the FILE menu and select Exit.

APPLICATIONS

Use HELP for quick reference to the proper use of a *NetWare* command.

TYPICAL OPERATION

In this activity you use HELP to quickly review the proper use of the public command SEND. Begin at the DOS prompt of a logged-in workstation.

1. Type **HELP SEND** and press **Enter**. The screen looks similar to the following:

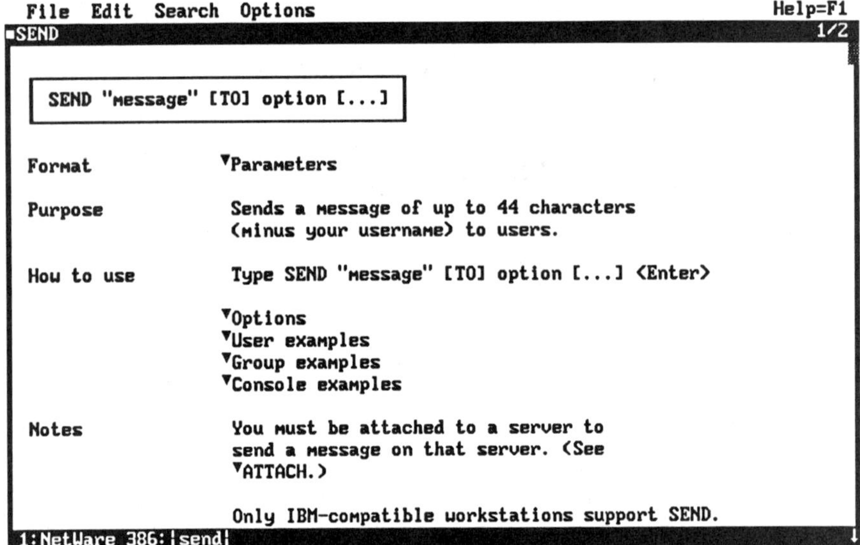

2. To exit HELP, press **Alt-F** and **Enter**. Select Exit by typing **E**, and press **Enter**.

3. Turn to Module 79 to continue the learning sequence.

Module 46
HIDEFILE
(ver 2.x and 3.x)

DESCRIPTION

The system command HIDEFILE flags specified files so they cannot be listed or deleted. Once hidden as such, files are no longer shown by the DOS DIR command. They cannot be erased by the DOS DELETE command, nor can they be overwritten with DOS COPY. Outside of this, however, the files are still useable.

You follow the command by the name of the file to hide. You can precede the filename with its path (drive specification and directory name) if different from the current path. You can also use wild cards (* and ?) in specifying the filename(s).

APPLICATIONS

HIDEFILE can be used to prevent other users from knowing of a file's existence. This is a simple way of keeping certain users out of applications or data for security reasons. It is also used to protect files from being accidentally erased or changed. The system command SHOWFILE restores files to their normal status (see Module 83).

TYPICAL OPERATION

In this activity you hide and protect a file named "TEST.TXT." Begin at the DOS prompt of a logged-in workstation.

1. Type **HIDEFILE TEST.TXT** and press **Enter**. Note the display:

```
F:\INN>HIDEFILE TEST.TXT
MAIN/SYS: INN
        TEST.TXT        hidden

F:\INN>
```

2. Type **DIR TEST.TXT** and press **Enter**. Note the display:

```
F:\INN>DIR TEST.TXT

 Volume in drive F is SYS
 Volume Serial Number is 9901-7CD9
 Directory of F:\INN

File not found

F:\INN>
```

3. Turn to Module 83 to continue the learning sequence.

Module 44
HOLDOFF
(ver 2.x and 3.x)

DESCRIPTION

HOLDOFF is a system command used to release a file previously locked by HOLDON (see Module 45). It reinstates a file's ability to be accessed by several users at once. It also restores the file's ability to be printed. The syntax is:

```
HOLDOFF
```

APPLICATIONS

When you are finished using an application which was protected from other users by the HOLDON command, execute HOLDOFF.

TYPICAL OPERATION

In this activity you unlock a file previously locked by HOLDON (see Module 45). Begin at the DOS prompt of a logged-in workstation.

1. Type **HOLDOFF** and press **Enter**. Note the display returns to your DOS prompt.
2. Turn to Module 50 to continue the learning sequence.

Module 45
HOLDON
(ver 2.x and 3.x)

DESCRIPTION

HOLDON is a system command which locks other users out of any files that you open until you release them with HOLDOFF. Users may read these files but cannot modify them. Also, while the file is locked, it cannot be sent to the printer. The syntax is:

```
HOLDON
```

APPLICATIONS

Applications written specifically for network use allow several users simultaneous access to the same files. These programs must lock files (or records) while a given user is making changes. Otherwise, the first user's changes may be overwritten by the second user. If a program is not designed to handle such data locking, and yet the program is shareable (more than one user can run the program at once), data loss or corruption can occur. By executing the HOLDON command on a program file before using it, other users cannot gain access to the file until the HOLDOFF command is issued.

Unfortunately, this also keeps you from being able to print the locked file. Therefore, you must exit the file and run HOLDOFF before printing it.

TYPICAL OPERATION

Suppose you are on a large or spread out network and need to use an application which is shareable but does not provide file or record locking. To make sure that no other users access the application until you are through with it, perform the following steps. Begin at the DOS prompt of a logged-in workstation.

1. Type **HOLDON** and press **Enter**. Notice the display returns to the DOS prompt.
2. Be sure to use HOLDOFF (see Module 44) to release the application to others.
3. Turn to Module 44 to continue the learning sequence.

Module 46
INSTALL
(ver 3.x)

DESCRIPTION

INSTALL is a *NetWare* Loadable Module (NLM, see Module 6) that is used to install and modify 3.x fileservers. The main menu of INSTALL is broken down into four sets of options.

DISK OPTIONS

FORMAT is used to perform a low level format on fileserver hard drives. This, of course, destroys any existing data. Many drives come already formatted. These include IDE, SCSI, and any drives designated *"NetWare* Ready." Even drives that are not preformatted, such as some MFM and ESDI drives, are usually formatted with routines built into the drive controller or the system BIOS. Refer to the installation manual of the drive for specific directions, or consult a network integrator.

PARTITION TABLES allows you to create or delete *NetWare* partitions. When a new hard drive is added to the fileserver, create a partition for it. The HOTFIX feature under this menu allows you to view or invoke this built-in feature to *NetWare*. HOTFIX constantly monitors everything written to a drive, reading back and confirming each block of data. If a given block cannot be read back or the data is corrupt, HOTFIX marks that block defective and redirects future reads for it to a reserve area. The amount of reserve still available for a drive can be checked periodically. If the reserve is going down unusually quickly, it is probably a sign of a hard drive about to fail!

NOTE
When a *NetWare* partition is deleted, all data is permanently lost!

MIRRORING, like HOTFIX, is a part of *NetWare*'s System Fault Tolerance. With mirroring, two identical drives are installed in the fileserver. One is selected as the primary drive, and *NetWare* maintains a constant duplicate of all of its data on the second drive. If either drive fails, its mirror continues to operate normally. The network administrator can then schedule downtime for a network integrator to replace the defective drive. Thus, emergency downtime as well as lost data is averted.

SURFACE TEST, like FORMAT, is typically not used. In the earlier days of *NetWare*, today's degree of SFT was not available. Further, hard drives were not as dependable.

Under these circumstances, it was important to thoroughly test the drive and mark any bad areas that the factory missed. On large drives this process can take many hours! Drives can still be tested (*NetWare* calls the process COMPSURF), but they generally are not.

VOLUME OPTIONS

This option lists any existing *NetWare* volume. To view information about a volume, highlight it and press Enter. To create new volumes, use Ins. Each *NetWare* volume, once mapped, appears to network users as a single separate hard drive. In reality, a single hard drive can be split into one or more partitions. Each partition can be a separate volume. Or a volume partition (under 3.x) can span several partitions and hard drives.

NOTE
When a *NetWare* volume is deleted, all data is permanently lost!

For each volume, you must assign a unique name. It is this name that you will use, with the MAP public command (Module 52), to assign a drive letter to the volume. You specify the size of the volume, choosing one or more segments from unallocated partitions. Once a volume is created, it is made available to network users via the console command MOUNT (Module 56).

SYSTEM OPTIONS

COPY SYSTEM AND PUBLIC FILES is only used during the initial installation. At least the first volume (always named SYS) must have been defined and MOUNTed. This option copies all of the system and public commands and utilities into the appropriate directories on this volume. These are executed from users at their workstations. It is to these commands and utilities that this book devotes the majority of itself.

CREATE AUTOEXEC.NCF provides a quick and easy way of recording the current fileserver setup. Information concerning the hard drive controller(s), network interface card(s) (NICs), fileserver name and address, and other pertinent data is placed in a file named AUTOEXEC.NCF in the SYS:SYSTEM directory. Thereafter, when the fileserver is booted and SYS is mounted, these commands are executed, and the fileserver bootup is automated. Note, though, that you cannot MOUNT SYS without having loaded the hard drive controller driver for the hard drive that contains this volume; therefore, the need for the next option.

CREATE STARTUP is similar to AUTOEXEC.NCF in that it automates server bootup. However, it resides on the boot drive of the fileserver (floppy drive A or a hard drive DOS partition). The one mandatory command here is that which loads and configures the driver for the hard drive that contains volume SYS. Thereafter, AUTOEXEC.NCF takes over. Once again, this option will create the file based on the current setup.

EDIT AUTOEXEC.NCF allows you to make changes to this file once it is created.

EDIT STARTUP allows you to make changes to this file.

APPLICATIONS

INSTALL provides all of the functions necesary to install and maintain *NetWare* 3.x on a fileserver.

TYPICAL OPERATION

While the functionality of INSTALL is explained above, and its menu-driven environment is fairly straightforward, it does deal with complex technology. Further, misuse of certain INSTALL options can destroy large amounts of data, down the server without warning, and render the network unusable until a knowledgable network technician reverses the damage. Use INSTALL only if you fully understand it and only with the assistance of the *NetWare* installation manuals or a network integrator.

In this exercise, simply load the INSTALL NLM, then exit! Begin at the ":" prompt of a 3.x fileserver (running SERVER).

1. Type **LOAD INSTALL** and press **Enter**. The screen will resemble:

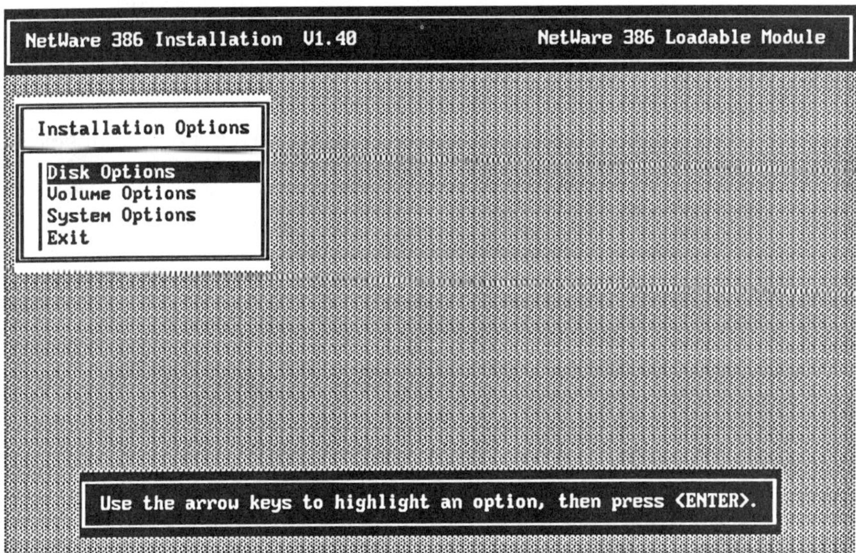

2. Exit INSTALL by pressing **Esc** and then **Enter**.
3. Turn to Module 13 to continue the learning sequence.

Module 47
LISTDIR
(ver 2.x and 3.x)

DESCRIPTION

LISTDIR is a public command which lists directories that are part of the named directory. If you do not specify a directory, the current default is assumed. LISTDIR is in some ways similar to the DOS TREE command. Additional information is listed by including the following flags, separated from the command by a backslash (\) and a space. You can use the full names or the abbreviations.

A (All)

This flag displays all information available with LISTDIR. This is the same as including all three of the following flags.

D (Date)

This flag displays the date and time that each listed directory was created.

E (Effective rights)

This flag displays your actual rights or privileges in each directory (see Module 76).

R (Rights)

This flag displays your maximum rights or privileges in each directory (see Module 76).

S (Subdirectories)

This flag causes all directories "below" the specified directory to be included in the listing.

APPLICATIONS

Use LISTDIR to determine the existence and location of various directories. LISTDIR is also an easy way of determining your current rights in all directories.

TYPICAL OPERATION

In this activity you use LISTDIR to display all directories immediately below the current default, as well as when each directory was created. Begin at the DOS prompt of a logged-in workstation.

1. Type **LISTDIR\ D** and press **Enter**. The screen resembles this:

```
 5-11-90    4:55p  MIKUS
 3-27-89    6:08p  SK
 3-27-89    6:32p  WESTECH
 3-27-89    6:34p  FORMS
 7-19-89    1:47p  TWO
 3-18-91    4:08p  LOTSHARE
 2-07-91    2:30p  HOTLIST
 6-06-89    5:38p  SOP
 3-28-91    2:51p  DMS
 2-26-91    9:43a  GUEST
 7-08-91   12:26p  BOB
 4-15-91    4:34p  TMP
 4-18-91    4:34p  RCIA
 5-31-91   11:20a  DOS
 6-05-91    9:34a  RICH
 3-01-91    3:50p  BYRON
 3-04-91   10:47a  RAY
10-07-91   10:23a  BRAD
11-06-91    3:28p  AMI
 7-08-91   12:29p  BROOKS
 7-11-91    8:01p  BSMS
 7-24-91   11:28a  WALLY
72 sub-directories found
```

2. Try this command using other flags or directories as well.

3. Turn to Module 74 to continue the learning sequence.

Module 48
LOGIN
(ver 2.x and 3.x)

DESCRIPTION

The public command LOGIN establishes you as a user on a given fileserver. You must "LOGIN" using a valid *username* as created by the network supervisor (see SYSCON, Module 86). You must also know the password, if any, assigned to that username. *NetWare* does not distinguish between uppercase and lowercase; usernames and passwords can be entered either way. If you enter an invalid username, *NetWare* still asks for a password; regardless of what is entered at this point, *NetWare* responds with "ACCESS DENIED."

On networks with more than one fileserver, it is important to specify to which server you wish to log in. This is done by preceding the username with a valid fileserver name and a forward slash (/). To shorten this process you can enter the fileserver name (if different from the default) and the username immediately following the LOGIN command. It is possible for more than one user to have concurrent access to a fileserver using the same username. This, however, can cause confusion when listing current users and sending messages (see USERLIST and SEND, modules 90 and 79, respectively).

Upon successful execution of the LOGIN command, *NetWare* invokes the appropriate *login script* defined by the SYSCON utility (see modules 50 and 86). Login scripts define search paths and may run commands or programs in a fashion similar to the DOS *AUTOEXEC.BAT* file.

There are three flags that can be included in the LOGIN command.

Flag	*Name and Purpose*
S	Script flag indicates that you wish to invoke a different login script. Both system and individual login scripts are skipped, and the one specified is executed.
NA	No Attach flag is used when you are already attached to one or more fileservers. You do not want to LOGOUT from them, but you do wish to execute a login script that resides on one of them (or another server). This would be typically used with a fairly complicated drive mapping environment that requires

considerable change when switching from one task to another (see MAP, Module 52).

C   Clear screen causes the workstation screen to clear as soon as your password is typed in.

The syntax for the LOGIN command is:

```
LOGIN flags fileservername/username optional_login_script
```

Replace flags with any desired flags. Fileservername is only required on multiserver networks. Optional_login_script is only needed when the S or NA flags are used. It should be the complete path for the optional login script file.

APPLICATIONS

After booting your workstation and attaching to the network using ANETx.COM or IPX.COM or NETx.COM (see Module 10), use the LOGIN command to gain access to the files on a given fileserver. The specific resources which you may access (volumes, directories, printers, etc) and the ways in which you may affect them (Read, Write, Erase, etc.) are established by the network administrator or workgroup managers. When you are finished with your work on that fileserver, use the LOGOUT command.

TYPICAL OPERATION

In this operation you use the LOGIN command to attach your workstation to a fileserver. This example assumes your username to be FRED, with the password SUNSHINE. Begin at the DOS prompt.

1. Boot your workstation onto the network (see Module 8).

2. Switch to the first network drive. On a typical Novell network this is drive F. Type **F:** and press **Enter.**

   You are now in a directory called LOGIN which contains the file LOGIN.COM. Any attempt to change directories or access other files will fail until you have logged in.

3. Type **LOGIN** and press **Enter.**

4. Type **FRED** and press **Enter.**

   If you have been assigned a password, you are now prompted to enter it.

5. Type **SUNSHINE** and press **Enter.** The screen resembles:

```
F:\>LOGIN
Enter your login name: ACCTG/FRED
Enter your password:
Drive  F: = MAIN\SYS:   \
Drive  H: = MAIN\SYS:   \USERS\FRED
Drive  G: = MAIN\VOL1:  \
Drive  I: = MAIN\SYS:   \TRAINING
Drive  L: = MAIN\SYS:   \WINDOWS
SEARCH1:  = Z:. [TECH\SYS:   \PUBLIC]
SEARCH2:  = Y:. [TECH\SYS:   \PUBLIC\IBM_PC\V5.00]
SEARCH3:  = X:. [TECH\SYS:   \WINDOWS]
SEARCH4:  = W:. [TECH\SYS:   \UTILITES]
SEARCH5:  = V:. [TECH\VOL1:  \LANSIGHT]

F:\>
F:\>
```

6. Turn to Module 49 to continue the learning sequence.

Module 49
LOGOUT
(ver 2.x and 3.x)

DESCRIPTION

The public command LOGOUT cancels your ability to access the files on a specified fileserver. This counteracts the LOGIN command and the effects of login scripts. Network access is not disabled by LOGOUT, but you are switched to the LOGIN directory on the default drive and all other drives mapped to that fileserver are no longer accessible. On single-server networks it is not necessary to specify the server name. If the server name is omitted on multiserver networks, you are logged out of all fileservers to which you had access.

APPLICATIONS

After completing your work on a given server, use the LOGOUT command to cancel your ability to access that server's files. By logging out before leaving your workstation, you prevent others from unauthorized access of network files.

TYPICAL OPERATION

In this activity you release your ability to access a fileserver. Begin at the DOS prompt of a logged-in workstation.

1. Type **LOGOUT** and press **Enter**. Your screen resembles this:

```
F:\>LOGOUT
FRED logged out from server MAIN connection 2.
Login time:   Tuesday January 1, 1992   8:55 PM
Logout time:  Tuesday January 1, 1992   8:56 PM


F:\LOGIN>
```

2. To log out of a particular fileserver, ACCT, type **LOGOUT ACCT** and press **Enter.**

3. Turn to Module 81 to continue the learning sequence.

Module 50
LOGIN SCRIPTS
(ver 2.x and 3.x)

DESCRIPTION

The *login script* is a set of instructions which is carried out by *NetWare* when a user logs in. The concept is similar to that of the DOS AUTOEXEC.BAT file. You create and modify login scripts through the SYSCON menu utility (see Module 86). There is a *system login script* which is executed when any user logs in, and there are *user login scripts* which only affect the user for which they were created. You can also define alternate login scripts which are accessed with the LOGIN command (Module 48). The following are valid login script instructions:

#	Place the pound sign in front of the filename for any existing command file or executable file (those with extensions of .COM or .EXE). The named file will be executed with each login. Unlike DOS AUTOEXEC.BAT files, additional files with the extension .BAT cannot be called.
ATTACH	Use this the same as the PUBLIC command of the same name (Module 10). It allows a user to be automatically logged in to multiple fileservers.
BREAK ON/OFF	Place this instruction at the beginning of the login script to enable (BREAK ON) or disable (BREAK OFF) the user's ability to halt the login script by using Ctrl-C or Ctrl-Break. The default is BREAK OFF.
COMSPEC	Many applications require that DOS reload the COMMAND. COM file upon exiting them. Use the COMSPEC instruction to point to the location of this file. This prevents DOS from having to go back to the local drive from which you booted. An example of this command is:

```
COMSPEC = SYS:DOS\COMMAND.COM
```

DISPLAY/FDISPLAY	Use this instruction to cause the contents of a specified file to be displayed at the time of login. DISPLAY is used with standard text files; FDISPLAY is used with formatted files.

DOS BREAK ON/OFF	This is similar to the DOS command BREAK. Use DOS BREAK ON to enable the user to break out of applications by pressing Ctrl-C or Ctrl-Break. The default is DOS BREAK OFF.
DOS SET	Use this instruction to assign values to environmental variables. It is equivalent to the DOS SET command.
DOS VERIFY ON/OFF	Use DOS VERIFY ON to cause *NetWare* to verify files that are copied using NCOPY or FILER (Modules 58 and 38). Its effect is similar to that of the DOS command SET VERIFY ON used with the DOS COPY command. The default is DOS VERIFY OFF.
DRIVE	Use this to select which will be your current drive upon logging in. An example is: `DRIVE G:` The default is the first drive on the fileserver.
EXIT	Use this instruction to cause an immediate exit from the login script. If EXIT is followed by a filename with an extension of .EXE, .COM, or .BAT, that file will be executed.
FIRE PHASERS	Use this strange instruction to cause a "ray gun" sound effect. The phasers can be fired up to 9 times per instruction. An example is: `FIRE PHASERS 3 TIMES`
INCLUDE	Use this instruction to nest additional instructions within a login script. Put the additional instructions in a text file whose name follows INCLUDE. An example is: `INCLUDE SYS:INN\MORESTUFF.TXT`
MACHINE NAME	This assigns a machine name, as required with certain NETBIOS-compatible programs. With most applications it is not necessary.
MAP	Use this the same way as the PUBLIC command of the same name (Module 52). This instruction is usually used several times in a login script.
PAUSE	This has the same effect as the DOS command of the same name. Operation is halted until a key is pressed.

REMARK	This tells *NetWare* to ignore the balance of the instruction line. It is useful for adding comments to the login script.
WRITE	Follow this instruction with a message, enclosed in quotes, that you want displayed at the time of login. You can also WRITE *login variable* (see the following discussion). Separate multiple messages and variables by semicolons. A semicolon at the very end of the instruction causes the WRITE to be displayed on a single line. An example is:

```
WRITE "HELLO, "; LOGIN_NAME;
```

A login script can have an "IF THEN" program control, not unlike that used in many programming languages. An example is:

```
IF LOGIN_NAME="FRED" THEN
        DISPLAY SYS:FRED\HELLO.TXT
```

LOGIN_NAME is one of 22 *login variables*. They can be used as is, or as part of a text string if preceded with %. For example, to INCLUDE a text file called LOGIN.TXT located in a directory named after each user, you can use:

```
INCLUDE SYS:%LOGIN_NAME\LOGIN.TXT
```

The login variables are:

User-Related Variables

LOGIN_NAME	The username used to login.
FULL_NAME	The full name, if any, as assigned in SYSCON.
NEW_MAIL	The value is *YES* or *NO* and can be checked with "IF THEN." This indicates if the user has unread mail. An example is:

```
IF NEW_MAIL="YES" THEN WRITE "YOU HAVE NEW MAIL"
```

Workstation-Related Variables

STATION	The workstation number.
P_STATION	The workstation physical connection number.
MACHINE	The type of machine for which the workstation shell was generated.
SMACHINE	The short version of the machine name.
OS	The operating system with which the workstation was booted.
OS_VERSION	The version of the workstation's operating system.

Time-Related Variables

SECOND	Seconds, according to the current system time.
MINUTE	Minutes, according to the current system time.
HOUR	The current hour, according to the system time.
HOUR24	The current time in 24-hour format. (2:00 P.M. is 14:00).
GREETING_TIME	If the hour is midnight to noon, the value is *morning*; noon to 5:00 P.M. is *afternoon*, and 5:00 to midnight is *evening*.
AM_PM	The value is *AM* or *PM*.
MONTH	The current month number, 1-12.
MONTH_NAME	The name of the current month.
DAY_OF_WEEK	The day of the week, Sunday through Saturday.
DAY	The day of the month, 1-31.
NDAY_OF_WEEK	The numerical day of the week, 1 (Sunday) -7 (Saturday).
YEAR	The current year in 4 digits.
SHORT_YEAR	The current year in 2 digits.

The network administrator may not wish to let users modify their own login scripts. Novice users may have difficulty with some of the concepts used in login scripts, and therefore may be prone to mistakes that can leave their working environment unusable. At any rate, the system login script is only for modification by administrators, and therefore cannot be accessed without supervisor privileges.

APPLICATIONS

A login script can be defined for each user according to his or her special needs. In simple networks where you use the same basic applications, user login scripts may not be necessary. A system login script giving all users the same basic working environment should suffice. However, with many networks you may wish to map drives and search paths according to your individual needs, as well as establish login greetings according to your desires.

TYPICAL OPERATION

Login scripts are created using SYSCON and MAKEUSER (modules 86 and 51).

Turn to Module 86 to continue the learning sequence.

Module 51
MAKEUSER
(ver 2.x and 3.x)

DESCRIPTION

MAKEUSER allows you to create or delete users in batches. SYSCON (Module 86) provides an easy, menu-driven way to create users one at a time. However, if you need to create several users with similar definitions, MAKEUSER can save you a great deal of time. The MAKEUSER utility processes a text file in which a set of instructions defines the users to be created. MAKEUSER has a built-in editor for creating this file, or you can use any application that will create text files. You must give the file a .USR extension. Begin each new instruction line in the file with #. These are the valid instructions for use in a MAKEUSER file:

User Definition Instructions

ACCOUNT_
EXPIRATION

This is used only when the SYSCON accounting option is active. Follow the instruction by a valid date on which this user account is to expire. The default is "no expiration date."

ACCOUNTING

This is used only when the SYSCON accounting option is active. Follow the instruction by the opening number of accounting units available to this user, and the lowest level the account will be allowed. An example is:

```
#ACCOUNTING 5000, 0
```

CONNECTIONS

This limits the number of workstations a user may be logged into at once. Since a fileserver has a limit of 100 concurrent connections, the values are 1-100. The default is "no limit." An example is:

```
#CONNECTIONS 2
```

GROUPS

Follow this instruction by a list of valid GROUP names to which the user(s) will belong. An example is:

```
#GROUPS ACCTG; MNGMNT; SALES
```

HOME_DIRECTORY   This specifies a valid directory name in which to create the user(s) home directories. These directories have the same name as the username.

LOGIN_SCRIPT   This instruction tells MAKEUSER where to find a text file containing the login script to be used for the user(s) being created.

MAX_DISK_SPACE   This limits the number of 4-kilobyte disk blocks that the user(s) will be allowed to use. An example is:

```
#MAX_DISK_SPACE 5000
```

PASSWORD_
LENGTH   This instruction is only valid when preceded by the PASSWORD_REQUIRED instruction. It establishes a minimum length for user passwords. The default, when a password is required, is 5.

PASSWORD_
PERIOD   This, too, is only valid when preceded by the PASSWORD_REQUIRED instruction. It sets the number of days between forced password changes. To force users to change their password about once a month, use:

```
#PASSWORD_PERIOD 30
```

PASSWORD_
REQUIRED   This instruction requires the created user(s) to use passwords.

PURGE_USER_
DIRECTORY   This instruction is only valid when user(s) are being deleted. It causes the subdirectories owned by the users to be deleted.

RESTRICTED_TIME   This defines times when created user(s) cannot log in to the fileserver. The term *EVERYDAY* can be used to indicate every day of the week. To keep these users out from 8:00 p.m. to midnight on Thursdays and Fridays, use:

```
#RESTRICTED_TIME THURSDAY, 8:00 PM, 12:00 AM;
FRIDAY, 8:00 PM, 12:00 AM
```

STATIONS   This limits the workstations from which users can log in to the fileserver. You must specify both network and workstation node address. These are hexadecimal numbers established at the time of network installation.

UNIQUE_
PASSWORD   This is only valid when the PASSWORD_REQUIRED instruction precedes it. This instruction makes created user(s) always select a password that is unique from any of the past 8 passwords they have used.

Makeuser Control Instructions

CLEAR — This clears all values set by the USER DEFINITION INSTRUCTIONS. Use it as follows:

```
#CLEAR
```

CREATE — This instruction tells MAKEUSER to create a user according to any DEFINITION INSTRUCTIONS that precede. Follow CREATE by a username, full name, and passwords, separated by semicolons. To create the user FRED, with the full name of FRED FLINTSTONE, and a password of DINO, you would use:

```
#CREATE FRED; FRED FLINTSTONE; DINO
```

DELETE — This instruction tells MAKEUSER to delete a user. You can specify several users, separating their usernames with semicolons. To delete user FRED:

```
#DELETE FRED
```

APPLICATIONS

On small networks, users are often created and defined one at a time. With MAKEUSER, an administrator of a large LAN can save a considerable amount of time by creating users with similar definitions in batches.

TYPICAL OPERATION

This file creates users FRED SMITH and MARY SMITH with the passwords SUNSHINE and MOONLIGHT, respectively. They are limited to using one workstation each at a time. They cannot use the network on Friday night. A password will always be required for these users. Begin at the DOS prompt of a logged-in workstation.

1. Type **MAKEUSER** and press **Enter**. The MAKEUSER main menu appears.
2. Use the Arrow keys to highlight "Create New USR File." Press **Enter**.
3. Type the following text. Press **Enter** at the end of each line.

```
#CONNECTIONS 1
#RESTRICTED TIME FRIDAY, 7:00 PM, 12:00 AM
#PASSWORD REQUIRED
#CREATE FRED, FRED SMITH, SUNSHINE
#CREATE MARY, MARY SMITH, MOONLIGHT
```

4. Press **Esc,** then type **Y** to conclude this file.

   You are now prompted to enter a name for this file.

5. Type **NEWUSERS** and press **Enter**.

6. Using the Arrow keys, select "Process USR File." The users are created.

7. Press **Esc**, then **Y** to exit "Process USR File."

8. Press **Alt-F10**, then **Y** to exit MAKEUSER.

9. Turn to Module 80 to continue the learning sequence.

Module 52
MAP
(ver 2.x and 3.x)

DESCRIPTION

The public command MAP assigns drive names (A through Z) to *NetWare* directories. This is probably one of the most important *NetWare* commands, because without it the fileserver's volumes cannot be accessed.

While drive names can be any letter, A-Z, you should not use letters already assigned to local drives in your workstation (such as A for your first floppy drive). If you do, you can no longer access these local drives, until they are mapped back or you log out of the fileserver.

Under DOS 3.0 and above, DOS reserves drive names A-E for local use. Therefore, start with F for *NetWare* drive mapping. When *NetWare* is first installed, the default is to map the first available drive (F: under DOS 3.0 and above) to the SYS: volume's root directory. Thus, on a newly installed network with your workstation running DOS 3.0 and above, you can access the volume SYS: by typing F: and pressing Enter.

The syntax for MAP is:

```
MAP drive_name flag = Vol: Directory
```

When MAP is used to drive names as such, you can use the command without a flag, or replace *flag* with any of these four flags:

Flag	*Effect*
DEL	The DELete flag removes the drive mapping previous established with this drive_name.
N	The Next flag determines the next available drive_name alphabetically and uses it for this drive mapping.
ROOT	ROOT makes the drive mapping appear to be the root (highest level) directory for the drive_name. This is useful for applications that require being installed in the root directory of a drive. This command is similar to the DOS command SUBST.

INS   Insert is similar to Next. It determines the next available Search drive_name (numerically) and uses it to establish a Search Path to that directory. Search Paths are explained below.

MAP can also be used to provide automatic searching through different directories for programs files. These files must have an extension of .COM, .EXE, or .BAT. In this function, MAP is similar in effect to the DOS command PATH. When used to establish search paths the command syntax is:

```
MAP SEARCHx: = VOL: Directory
```

SEARCH can be abbreviated with S. X is a number 1-16 that designates the order in which the directories will be searched. When you attempt to run a program *NetWare* looks for it first in the current default directory, then in each SEARCH path in numerical order. If the program is not found in any of these, then the message "BAD COMMAND OR FILENAME" is displayed. Unlike the DOS PATH command, previously established search paths are not cancelled each time the command is issued.

NOTE

Issuing the DOS command PATH will negate any established MAP search paths. The MAP command can only designate a maximum of 26 drives. In other words, the number of drive names used plus the number of search paths established cannot exceed 26.

APPLICATIONS

You must establish drive names before you can access *NetWare* directories. Even though assigning drive F: to the SYS: volume root directory will give you the ability to access its subdirectories (using the standard DOS CHDIR command), it is often more convenient to have a drive name assigned to each commonly used directory. Many users find the concepts of changing drives easier to understand than that of changing directories. Map search paths allow more efficient hard disk organization. Programs can reside in one directory, yet be accessed from multiple directories. For example, a word processing program can be located in a directory called SYS:WP. Each user can have his or her own directory in which documents are kept and run the word processor from that directory.

The MAP command may be issued from a login script (see Module 50). This will save you the trouble of typing routinely used drive mappings every time you log in. The default login script establishes search path S1 to the SYS:PUBLIC directory. This is why you can execute the PUBLIC commands regardless of which directory is the current default.

TYPICAL OPERATION

In this activity assign drive name P to the directory SYS:PRACTICE (as created in Module 10). Then change the default directory to SYS:PRACTICE by changing to drive P. Finally, verify that you are in the SYS:PRACTICE directory by running the GO.BAT program. Begin at the DOS prompt of a logged-in workstation.

1. Type **MAP P:=SYS:PRACTICE** and press **Enter**. Your screen shows:

```
F:\>MAP P:=SYS:PRACTICE



Drive  P: = MAIN\SYS:   \PRACTICE

F:\>
```

2. Type **P:** and press **Enter**.
3. Type **GO.BAT** and press **Enter**.

Now change back to drive F: and establish a search path to SYS:PRACTICE so that you can run GO.BAT without changing drives or directories. Use the search Path S5, as the others already point by default to other directories.

4. Type **F:** and press **Enter**.
5. Type **MAP S5:=SYS:PRACTICE** and press **Enter**.
6. Type **GO** and press **Enter**.

This command could also be "MAP S5=P:" since P: has been assigned to SYS:PRACTICE. *NetWare* will search the default directory, then any directories assigned to S1 through S4. Finally, it will find GO.BAT in the SYS:PRACTICE directory. The screen will resemble:

```
F:\>MAP S5:=SYS:PRACTICE

SEARCH5:  = M:. [MAIN\SYS:   \PRACTICE]

F:\>
```

Remember, these drive mappings will be lost once you log out at the network.

7. Turn to Module 85 to continue the learning sequence.

Module 53
MENU
(ver 2.x and 3.x)

DESCRIPTION

MENU is a public command that allows you to create custom menu-driven working environments. These have the same look as SYSCON, FILER, and *NetWare*'s other menu-driven utilities. Simply create a text file containing menu selections and the corresponding programs, and MENU will interpret it. The syntax is:

```
MENU filename
```

The filename normally has a .MNU extension. If a different extension is used, you must specify it when issuing the MENU command. The following is an example of the default menu provided with *NetWare* in the PUBLIC directory under the filename MAIN.MNU.

```
%Main Menu
System Configuration
SysCon
File Management
Filer
Session Management
Session
Queue Management
Pconsole
```

The first line is displayed at the top of the menu. It must be preceded with the %. This line can include additional information describing how the menu will be displayed. In this example:

```
%Main Menu,10,50,6
```

the menu is displayed with the upper right-hand corner positioned on the 10th row and 50th column on the screen, using color palette number 6 (see COLORPAL, Module 20).

Each menu entry is followed by the indented name of the corresponding application. This must be a filename with the extension of .EXE, .COM, or .BAT (in other words, in the above example, SYSCON refers to the program SYSCON.EXE). In the

following example, a selection is added to the main menu. It calls a submenu named
Other Utilities.

```
%Main Menu
System Configuration
     SysCon
File Management
     Filer
Session Management
     Session
Queue Management
     Pconsole
Other Utilities
     %Other Utilities
%Other Utilities
Monitor Fileserver
     Fconsole
Monitor Current Volume
     Chkvol
```

This submenu contains two additional selections. To run the first menu, you type
MENU MAIN and you see the following:

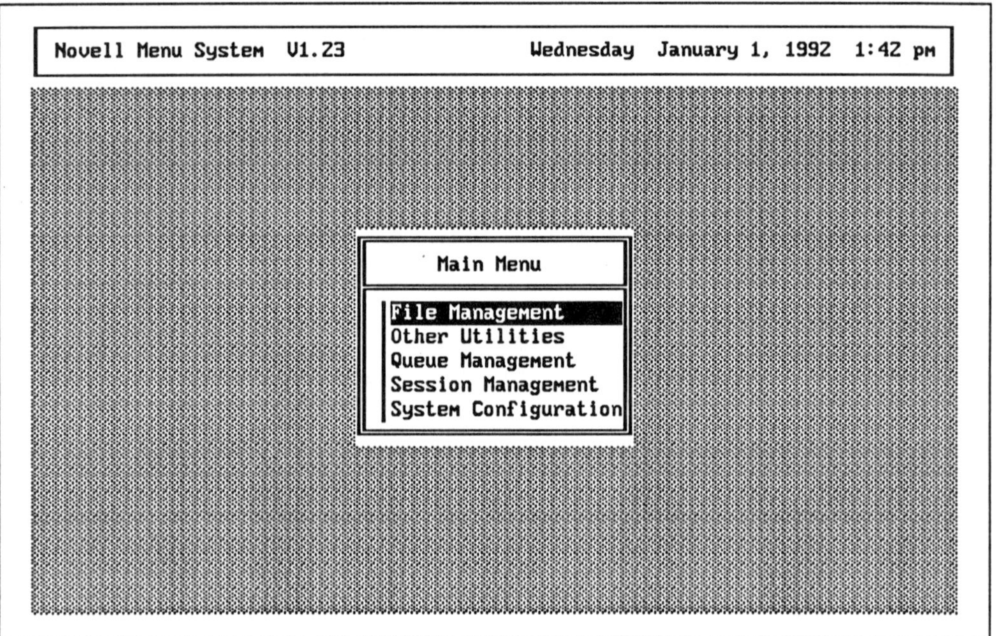

Notice that MENU puts the selections in alphabetical order. If you highlight (with the
Arrow keys) the Other Utilities selection and press **Enter**, the screen shows:

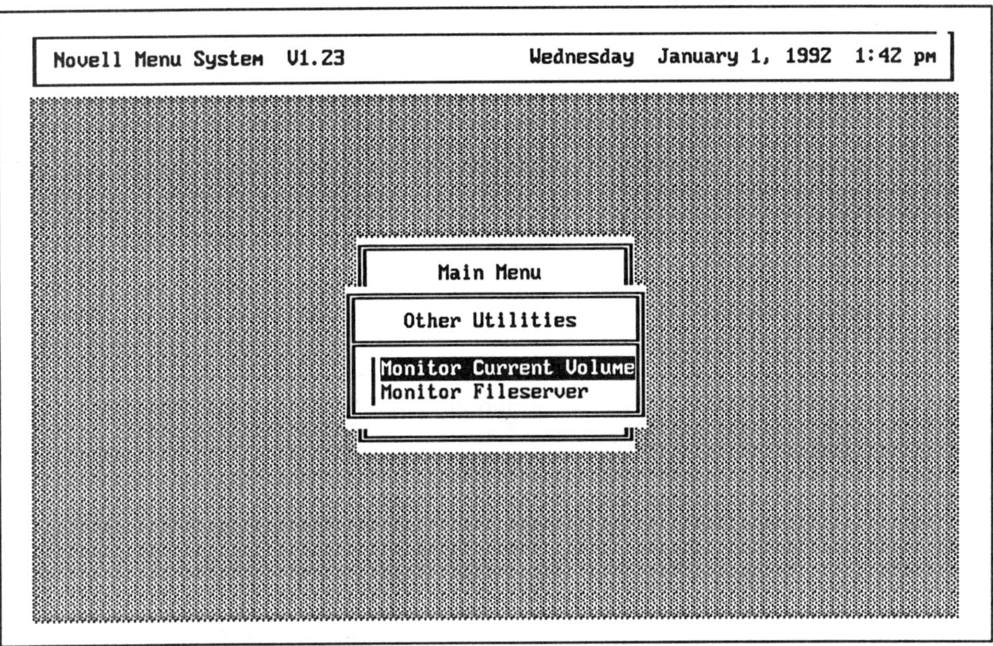

Note that the order of these two entries is opposite their order in the menu text file. MENU arranges entries alphabetically. As with all *NetWare* menu-driven utilities, you exit by pressing **Esc** until the Exit Menu box appears, then press **Enter**. You can also exit by pressing **Alt-F10** to go directly to the Exit Menu box.

APPLICATIONS

Many users prefer working in a menu-driven environment. This eliminates the need to memorize commands and the location of programs. Using MENU to provide a custom-built menu system, the administrator can structure the network so that users never have to issue commands from the workstation prompt.

TYPICAL OPERATION

In this activity you display the menu file MAIN.MNU that is located in the public directory. Begin at the DOS prompt of a logged-in workstation.

1. Type **MENU MAIN** and press **Enter**. A menu file similar to the one at the beginning of this module appears.

2. Exit by pressing **Esc**, then **Enter**.

3. Turn to Module 20 to continue the learning sequence.

Module 54
MONITOR
(ver 3.x)

DESCRIPTION

MONITOR is an NLM used to monitor a wide variety of information about users, file usage, network statistics, drive statistics, and the other NLMs currently being run. The main screen resembles the following:

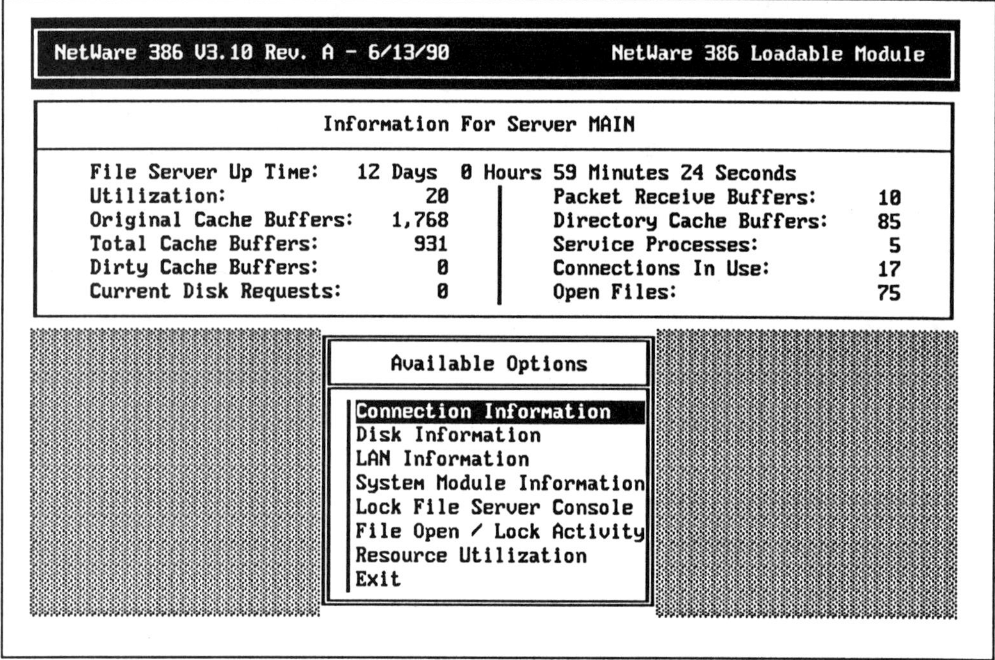

NOTE

If this or any other menu with MONITOR is left on the console display for too long, a "screen save" mechanism is invoked. It prevents the menu image from eventually "burning-in" the screen (leaving a permanent ghost image). MONITOR's screen save resembles a comet bouncing slowly around the screen. To return to the MONITOR menu, press any key.

CONNECTION INFORMATION displays each node currently attached to the fileserver. If a connection is highlighted, you can select it (with the Enter key) and view the files that the connection has open. If you highlight a connection and press Del, the node can be disconnected from the fileserver. This, of course, should only be done if you know that there is not a user with open files at that connection.

DISK INFORMATION provides extensive information about all disk channels. This includes disk space, caching statistics, and much more. Much of this is highly technical and only of importance to network technicians that are fine-tuning or troubleshooting a network.

LAN INFORMATION, like DISK INFORMATION, provides a wealth of technical data. Statistics for each network attached to the fileserver are reported.

SYSTEM MODULE INFORMATION lists all of the modules currently running on the fileserver.

LOCK FILE SERVER CONSOLE can be an important security feature. You type a password, and the console becomes locked. All keyboard entry is ignored until the correct password is typed in a second time. This prevents unauthorized users from performing potentially damaging operations at the fileserver.

FILE OPEN / LOCK ACTIVITY lets you select a volume, directory, and file. It then reports on the current use of that file.

RESOURCE UTILIZATION reports on how the many tasks that run as part of the 3.x fileserver operating system are using the fileserver's resources.

APPLICATIONS

Use MONITOR to monitor a wide variety of fileserver information. This can be accomplished from a workstation using MONITOR with RCONSOLE (Module 72).

TYPICAL OPERATION

In this activity you use the MONITOR NLM to view hard drive information. Begin at the ":" of a 3.x fileserver running SERVER.

1. Type **LOAD MONITOR** and press **Enter**.

2. Select DISK INFORMATION by using the Down Arrow, and then press **Enter**. The screen resembles this:

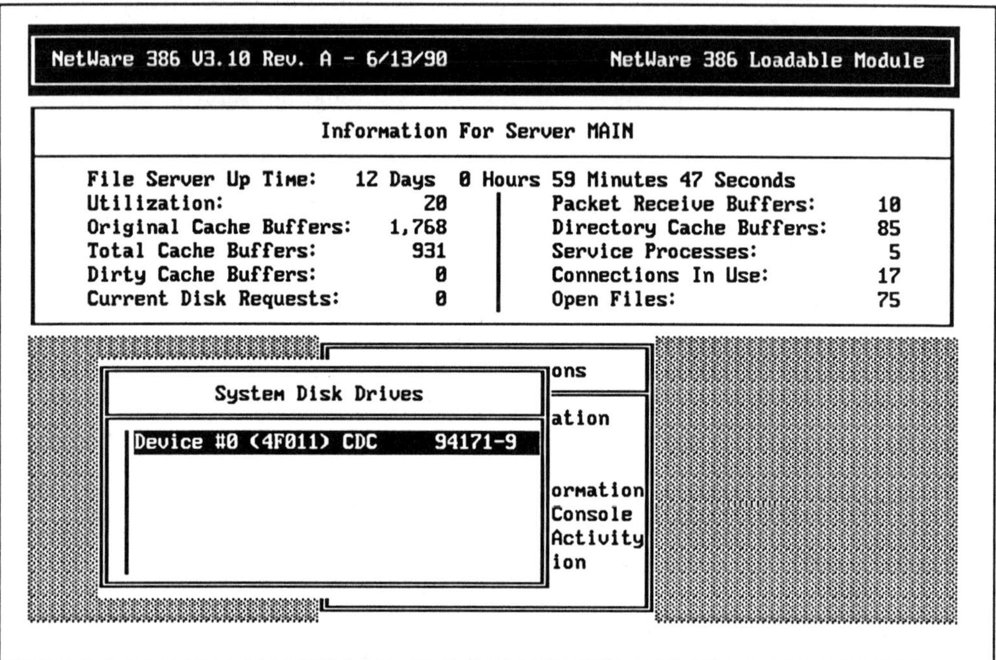

3. Turn to Module 57 to continue the learning sequence.

Module 55
MONITOR
(ver 2.x)

DESCRIPTION

MONITOR is a console command used to monitor the activities of the fileserver and any six logged-in (or attached) workstations.When you issue the command, the "monitor screen" is displayed. An NLM also called MONITOR (Module 54) provides this and more for *NetWare* 3.x users.

Across the top, the monitor screen displays the *NetWare* version in use, the utilization level (a percentage of the server's processing capacity currently in use), and the disk i/o pending (or number of cache blocks waiting to be written to disk). In addition, the following information is displayed for each of the six workstations being monitored:

Station #
Current Request
The last 5 filenames accessed

The current request represents the last fileserver request made by that workstation. Common requests include:

Begin transaction
Open File
Close File
Read File
Write File
Create File
Erase File
End Transaction
End of Job

This screen is automatically updated periodically. To force an immediate update of all activity, reissue the MONITOR command. To exit the monitor screen, use the console command OFF (see Module 62). The MONITOR command can be followed by the number of the first station to be displayed if other than stations 1-6. The screen will display the set of six workstations which start with the specified number.

APPLICATIONS

MONITOR provides a constant overview of network activity. The monitor screen is often left displayed while a console is not otherwise in use. Bear in mind that the constant updating of this screen takes up a small amount of fileserver processing time. MONITOR can help determine which users are accessing which files. It is useful in determining when all users have logged out in order to permit bringing down a fileserver. Also, use MONITOR to evaluate fileserver usage to determine if a given server is being too heavily accessed, thus slowing overall performance.

TYPICAL OPERATION

In this activity you display the monitor screen, including stations 1 through 6. Begin at the : prompt of your fileserver.

1. Type **MONITOR** and press **Enter**.

   Now shift the display to include stations seven through twelve. This may be done while the existing monitor screen is still running.

2. At the **:** below the monitor screen, type **MONITOR 7** and press **Enter**.

3. Turn to Module 62 to continue the learning sequence.

Module 56
MOUNT
(ver 2.x and 3.x)

DESCRIPTION

The console command MOUNT is used to inform *NetWare* to begin servicing a volume. A volume is a partition on a fileserver drive. The entire capacity of a drive can be allocated one volume, or it can be divided into several. Under *NetWare* 3.x, a volume can span more than one drive.

Under *NetWare* 2.x, this command is only used with fileservers that use removable media as a shared device. The fileserver caches the volume according to the installation parameters and makes it available to network users. If the removable volume is a pack of diskettes, use the MOUNT PACK version of the command. With either version, follow the command with the appropriate volume number. Nonremovable volumes are automatically mounted when the fileserver is booted, and dismounted when the fileserver is downed (Module 32).

With 3.x versions, *NetWare* must be told to mount and dismount volumes, even if they arc nonremovable. This can be done with manually typed commands, but typically volumes are mounted by the AUTOEXEC.NCF file (see Module 8), and dismounted by the DOWN command. The MOUNT ALL version of this command can be used to mount first the SYS volume and then any other defined and configured volumes on this fileserver.

APPLICATIONS

NetWare holds certain disk information in RAM memory. When changing removable media or replacing a hard drive, *NetWare* must be informed so that this cached information is written to disk and the volume is no longer accessible to users. Use MOUNT and DISMOUNT (see Module 28) to keep *NetWare* informed of such changes.

All volumes under 3.x must be mounted to make them available to network users. Because MOUNTed volumes take up fileserver RAM for caching, and fileserver performance is typically improved when more RAM is available to each volume, some administrators may choose to only MOUNT seldom used volumes when necessary.

TYPICAL OPERATION

In this activity you tell a *NetWare* 3.x fileserver to MOUNT all attached and configured volumes. Normally, this is done by the AUTOEXEC.NCF file, but it can also be done manually. This should not be performed without the supervision of a knowledgeable network administrator. Begin at the : prompt of your fileserver.

1. Type **DISMOUNT ALL** and press **Enter**.
2. Turn to Module 28 to continue the learning sequence.

Module 57
NAME
(ver 2.x and 3.x)

DESCRIPTION

The console command NAME is used to display the name assigned to a given fileserver. Under *NetWare* 2.x, fileservers are named at the time of *NetWare* installation. To change this name requires recentering the installation routine. *NetWare* 3.x allows the fileserver to be renamed easily by modifying the AUTOEXEC.NCF file. The next time the server is booted, the new name will be used.

APPLICATIONS

Many *NetWare* commands require you to know fileserver names. On large multiserver networks, you can use the NAME command to keep track of fileservers.

TYPICAL OPERATION

In this activity you display the name of the fileserver. Begin at the : of your fileserver.

1. Type **NAME** and press **Enter**. The fileserver name is displayed on your screen.

2. Turn to Module 22 to continue the learning sequence.

Module 58
NCOPY
(ver 2.x and 3.x)

DESCRIPTION

The public command NCOPY is similar to the DOS COPY command but with several advanced options. Because NCOPY operates on a fileserver level without having to channel a source file through your workstation and back to the server, it is usually much faster than using a DOS COPY. In naming the source and destination, you can specify the server name and directory name. If either of these is omitted, the current defaults are used. As with DOS COPY, you can use the "*" and "?" as wild cards. The following flags are valid with NCOPY:

Flag	Name	Description
A	ARCHIVE	Copy all indicated files that have their Archive bit set, which means that they have been modified since their last backup.
C	COPY	Copy as DOS files without retaining *NetWare* attributes or Name Space information.
F	FORCE	Force *NetWare* to write to sparse files.
I	INFORM	Inform user when non-DOS information will be lost during copy.
M	MODIFY	Copy Modified files and set their Archive bit off. This is used when NCOPY is used as a backup utility.
S	SUBDIRECTORIES	Include subdirectories in the NCOPY.
S/E	SUBS/EMPTY	Include even empty subdirectories in the NCOPY.

Each flag is preceded with the / character. The syntax of NCOPY is:

```
NCOPY Source_file(s) Target_file(s) Flags
```

APPLICATIONS

Use NCOPY to duplicate file(s) to a different directory, drive, or filename. NCOPY can be much quicker than COPY, particularly when copying multiple files or large files.

TYPICAL OPERATION

In this activity you make a copy of the file TEST.TXT in the SYS:INN directory. Keep the new file in the same directory, but name it NEWTEST.TXT. Tell *NetWare* to preserve the attributes. Begin at the DOS prompt of a logged-in workstation.

1. Type **NCOPY SYS:INN\TEST.TXT SYS:INN\NEWTEST.TXT /P** and press **Enter**. Your screen resembles the following:

```
F:\>NCOPY SYS:INN\TEST.TXT SYS:INN\NEWTEST.TXT /P
From MAIN/SYS:INN
To   MAIN/SYS:INN
     TEST.TXT        to NEWTEST.TXT

     1 file copied.

F:\>
```

2. Turn to Module 77 to continue the learning sequence.

Module 59
NDIR
(ver 2.x and 3.x)

DESCRIPTION

NDIR is a public command used to list the contents of directories. It provides extensive information about each item. It also gives the option to specify which items to include in the listing based on a number of criteria. The NDIR command is typically followed by a path and any of several flags. Under *NetWare* 2.x, when the command is used alone it lists all files in both the current directory and its subdirectories. The list includes the filename, the size (in bytes), the date and time of the last access and of the last modification to the file, the file's attributes, and the user that last modified the file. When used alone under 3.x, a simple menu system is displayed, allowing you to specify path and flags.

The path can include fileservers and volumes other than the current default, as well as the "*" and "?" wild card characters. The path can be followed by 25 different flags that determine which files will be listed and how they will be listed. Most of the flags have optional syntax that changes the way they are interpreted. The flags used to select files are as follows:

ACCESS=
The parameter is a date of the form MM-DD-YY. This flag includes all files that were last accessed on the parameter date.

Options: ACCESS BEFORE, ACCESS AFTER, ACCESS NOT BEFORE, ACCESS NOT AFTER.

CREATE=
The parameter is a date of the form MM-DD-YY. This flag includes all files that were created on the parameter date.

Options: CREATE BEFORE, CREATE AFTER, CREATE NOT BEFORE, CREATE NOT AFTER.

DIRECTORIESONLY (Or DO)
There are no parameters. This flag includes only directories, and not files, in the list.

Options: <none>.

FILENAME=   The parameter is a filename and can include the "*" and "?" as wild cards.

Options: FILENAME NOT =

FILESONLY=   There are no parameters. This flag includes files, but not directories, in the list.

Options: <none>.

OWNER=   The parameter is a username. This flag includes all files that were last accessed by this user.

Options: OWNER NOT.

SIZE=   The parameter is a number greater than 0. This flag includes all files whose size in bytes equals this number.

Options: SIZE GREATER THAN, SIZE LESS THAN, SIZE NOT GREATER THAN, SIZE NOT LESS THAN.

SUBDIRECTORIES   There are no parameters. This flag includes all subdirectories
(Or SUB)   of the current directory, but not files.

Options: <none>.

Files can also be selected based on their file attributes. With each of the attribute flags, you can precede the flag with the keyword "NOT." These attribute flags (and their abbreviations) include:

ExecutableOnly	EO
Hidden	H
Indexed	I
Modified	M
ReadOnly	RO
ReadWrite	RW
Shareable	SHA
System	SY
Transactional	T

Finally, there are two flags that determine how the list is displayed. The BRIEF flag lists only the filename, size, and last update for the listed files. The SORT flag sorts the list according to any of six different options. Each option can be preceded by the keyword "REVERSE" to cause the list to be sorted in reverse order. If you do not use the SORT option, files are listed in the order in which they appear in the directory. The SORT options are:

ACCESS | Sorts on date of last access.

CREATE | Sorts on date of file creation.

FILENAME | Sorts alphabetically by filename.

OWNER | Sorts alphabetically by the username of the last user to modify the file.

SIZE | Sorts numerically by the number of bytes the file occupies on the disk.

UPDATE | Sorts on date of last file modification.

Because this command has so many options, *NetWare* has provided one additional flag. This is HELP. Issue the NDIR HELP command for a review of NDIR options.

APPLICATIONS

NDIR is an invaluable tool in setting up and organizing network directories. Because many users often use one network drive, the number of files and directories can be very large and difficult to manage with the DOS command DIR. NDIR provides a sophisticated way to list file information.

TYPICAL OPERATION

In this activity you use NDIR to list extensive information about the files in the directory SYS:INN. Begin at the DOS prompt of a logged-in workstation.

1. Type **NDIR SYS:PUBLIC S*.*** and press **Enter**.

Now, list all the files (no subdirectories) in the SYS:PUBLIC directory that are greater than 15 kilobytes in size. Produce the list in alphabetical order according to filename.

2. Type **NDIR SYS:PUBLIC FILESONLY SIZE GREATER THAN=15000 SORT FILENAME** and press **Enter**.

3. Turn to Module 47 to continue the learning sequence.

Module 60
NPRINT
(ver 2.x and 3.x)

DESCRIPTION

The public command NPRINT allows you to transfer specified files directly to network printers. It is similar in concept to the DOS PRINT command. Like NCOPY, this command speeds execution by not routing the files through your workstation.

The files can reside on any available fileserver and can be sent to any network printer. You can use the "*" and "?" wildcards in naming files to be printed. The syntax is:

```
NPRINT path\filename printer number flag
```

The following flags control the way in which the files are printed. You can use the full name or the abbreviation of each one.

B= (Banner=)   The parameter is text, which can be up to twelve characters, and is printed on the banner page preceding the printout. The default is LST:.

C= (Copies=)   The parameter is the number of copies to print. The allowed range is 0 to 255. The default is 1.

D (Delete)   There are no parameters. If this flag is included, the specified file(s) are deleted after they are printed. The default is to not delete.

F= (Forms=)   The parameter is a name or number which specifies the type of form on which the file should be printed. For numbers, the allowed range is 0 to 255. Just before printing the file, the fileserver to which the target printer is attached verifies that the requested form is the same as the last one used on that printer. If not, a message is displayed asking that the appropriate form type be loaded.

The assignment of form type to form names and numbers is arbitrary. A list of available forms and their corresponding names and numbers should be established and provided to all users. Information concerning form types is established using PRINTDEF.

FF (Form Feed)	There are no parameters. This flag will force a form feed after your document is printed. This is the default mode.
J= (Job=)	The parameter is the name of the print job configuration you wish to use. Predefined configurations eliminate the need to specify many of the flags used with NPRINT. For a complete explanation of print job configurations, see PRINTCON in Module 65. The default is to not use a predefined configuration.
NAME=	The parameter is the username you wish to have printed on the banner page. Obviously, this flag is not valid when the NB flag is used. The default is to print your current username.
NB (No Banner)	There are no parameters. Include this flag to suppress the printing of a banner page before the file is printed. The default is to print banner pages.
NFF (No Form Feed)	There are no parameters. If the file being printed contains form feed commands, include this command to suppress additional automatic form feeds. The default is automatic form feeds.
NT (No Tabs)	There are no parameters. This flag causes tab characters to be ignored when printing the SPOOLed file. The default is to not ignore tabs.
Q= (Queue=)	The parameter is the name of the print queue you wish to receive this print job. The default is the first queue on the specified printer. If no printer, fileserver, and queue are specified, the print job will be sent to the current default server, printer 0, and queue PRINTQ_0.
S= (Server=)	The parameter is a text string naming any fileserver. This server is the target for the files to be printed. If the server has more than one printer attached, you can select one with the P flag or accept the default of 0). The server chosen does not have to be one to which you are currently logged in or attached. *NetWare* will temporarily log in to that server, print the files, and log back out. This procedure uses the GUEST username. If a password has been assigned to GUEST, you are prompted to enter it. If the GUEST username has been deleted, you are given the opportunity to log in using any other valid username. The default is the fileserver to which you are currently logged.

T= (Tabs=)   The parameter is the number of columns which separate the tabs in the files to be printed. The range is 0 to 18. If a file is generated by an application which uses a tab character instead of the appropriate number of spaces, the flag tells *NetWare* how to interpret the tabs. The default is 8.

APPLICATIONS

Use NPRINT to quickly add files to the print queue. These files are usually generated by applications which allow you to redirect printouts to disk storage. NPRINT provides a considerable amount of control over how the files are printed.

TYPICAL OPERATION

In this activity you send a file named TEST.TXT located in your current directory to a print queue named LASER, attached to your current default fileserver. In actual practice, of course, substitute an appropriate existing print queue name. Begin at the DOS prompt of a logged-in workstation.

1. Type **NPRINT TEST.TXT Q=LASER** and press **Enter**. The screen resembles this:

```
F:\INN>NPRINT TEST.TXT Q=LASER
Queuing data to Server MAIN, Queue LASER.
SYS:INN
        Queuing file TEST.TXT


F:\INN>
```

Next, send all files in the \INN directory with the .PRN extension to the same print queue. Suppress the banner page and print two copies of each file.

2. Type **NPRINT \INN*.PRN C2 NB Q=LASER** and press **Enter**. The screen should resemble this:

```
F:\>NPRINT \INN\*.PRN C2 NB Q=LASER
Queuing data to Server MAIN, Queue LASER.
SYS:INN
        Queuing file TEST.PRN


F:\>
```

Finally, send a file named TEST.TXT to queue EPSON on a fileserver named ACCTG. TEST.TXT is located in your current default directory. This file is to be printed on a form type number five. Delete the file after it is printed.

3. Type **NPRINT TEST.TXT SERVER=ACCTG Q=EPSON F=5 D** and press **Enter**. Notice the display:

```
F:\INN>NPRINT TEST.TXT SERVER=ACCTG Q=EPSON F=5 D
Queuing data to Server ACCTG, Queue EPSON.
SYS:INN
        Queuing file TEST.TXT

F:\INN>
```

4. Turn to Module 64 to continue the learning sequence.

Module 61
NSNIPES
(ver 2.x and 3.x)

DESCRIPTION

NSNIPES is a multiuser game provided with *NetWare*. It is located in the public directory. There are two versions: NSNIPES for monochrome displays, and NCSNIPES for color displays. The game allows one or more players to travel through a maze which is displayed on their monitors. Players are allowed five "lives" and score by shooting the "snipe" characters and the "factories." Movement and shooting are controlled as follows:

	Move	*Shoot*
Up	Up Arrow	W
Down	Down Arrow	S or X
Left	Left Arrow	A
Right	Right Arrow	D
Fast	Spacebar	

Combining certain keys allows moving and shooting at 45-degree angles. To play, all players must change to the same directory and must have READ, WRITE, OPEN, and CREATE privileges in that directory.

APPLICATIONS

Use NSNIPES to have fun, avoid work, and sharpen your hunting skills.

TYPICAL OPERATION

In this example you play NSNIPES using the \PUBLIC directory. Each player should follow these steps, beginning at the DOS prompt of a logged-in workstation.

1. Type **CD\PUBLIC** and press **Enter**.

2. If you are on a monochrome system, type **NSNIPES** and press **Enter**. On color, type **NCSNIPES** and press **Enter**.

    The first player to complete step 2 is prompted to press Enter again to start the game. Don't start until everyone has completed step 2.

3. Press **Ctrl-C** or **Ctrl-Break** to quit the game. The player who started the game should be the last one to quit. Otherwise, remaining players may have to reset their workstations to quit.

4. Turn to Module 43 to continue the learning sequence.

Module 62
OFF
(ver 2.x and 3.x)

DESCRIPTION

The console command OFF is the fileserver equivalent of the DOS command CLS. It simply clears the console screen. Under *NetWare* 2.x it also halts the MONITOR utility (see Module 55) and clears the DISK screen (see Module 27). The screen is cleared and the familiar : prompt is displayed in the upper right-hand corner.

APPLICATIONS

Use OFF to clear the monitor (or DISK) screen and allow the use of other console commands on 2.x fileservers or to simply clear the screen under 3.x.

TYPICAL OPERATION

In this activity you clear the monitor screen which you started in the Typical Operation of Module 55. Begin at the : prompt below the monitor screen.

1. Type **OFF** and press **Enter**.

   The screen clears and displays the normal console prompt (:).

2. Turn to Module 54 to continue the learning sequence.

Module 63
PAUDIT
(ver 2.x and 3.x)

DESCRIPTION

PAUDIT is a system command and is only valid on fileservers on which the *NetWare* "accounting" feature has been activated (using SYSCON, Module 86). All network activities being tracked by accounting are stored as entries in a file called SYS:SYSTEM\NET$ACCT.DAT. To conserve disk space, this file is compressed and cannot be directly read. PAUDIT reads this file and lists its information on your workstation display. If you want a hard copy of this report, use the DOS > PRN command to redirect output to the printer. After printing, you may wish to delete (perhaps after having backed up) the NET$ACCT.DAT file. If you do not, it continues to grow and can eventually waste a lot of disk space.

APPLICATIONS

NetWare "accounting" allows administrators to break down overall network usage among users or groups. This is useful in billing different departments for network use, as well as projecting future network needs and expansion. This information is reported using PAUDIT.

TYPICAL OPERATION

In this activity you print a report of all activity on the network that accounting has been tracking. Begin at the DOS prompt of a logged-in workstation.

1. To send the report to a local printer, ensure that the local printer port is not redirected to the network—type **ENDCAP** and press **Enter**. To direct the report to a network printer (in this case printer 0 on the default server), type **CAPTURE L=0 P=0** and press **Enter**. ENDCAP and CAPTURE are covered in modules 36 and 14.

2. Type **PAUDIT > PRN** and press **Enter**.

3. Turn to Module 88 to continue the learning sequence.

Module 64
PCONSOLE
(ver 2.x and 3.x)

DESCRIPTION

PCONSOLE is a menu-driven utility that allows you to create, monitor, modify, and delete print queues. A print queue holds print jobs and sends them to the designated printer one at a time. Print jobs are sent to the print queue by NPRINT (Module 60), CAPTURE (Module 14), or by applications written specifically for network printing. PCONSOLE also allows you to add print jobs directly to a queue, delete print jobs, or rearrange the order of print jobs. The main menu of PCONSOLE offers these selections:

> Change Current File Server
> Print Queue Information
> Print Server Information

The first selection simply allows you to choose from a list of available fileservers. The second allows you to choose from a list of existing print queues, or create and delete queues using the Insert and Delete keys. When a queue is created or selected, the following options become available:

Current Print Job Entries	This lists print jobs waiting in this queue. The Insert and Delete keys will add to or remove jobs from this list.
Current Queue Status	This displays information concerning the queue, including the number of entries currently in the queue or the number of fileservers (and print servers) attached. This also lets you enable or disable the queue's ability to accept additional print jobs, to send jobs to attached servers, and to allow additional servers to attach.
Currently Attached Servers	This lists all fileservers currently attached to this queue. Once again, use Insert or Delete to edit the list.
Print Queue ID	This displays the ID that is assigned to this queue.

Queue Operators	This lists all users who have been made operators of this particular queue. Only operators and supervisors have the ability to delete and rearrange print jobs. You can Insert and Delete operators.
Queue Servers	This lists print servers currently available to the queue. These can be fileservers or dedicated print servers.
Queue Users	This lists all users who are currently allowed to use this queue. Users or groups can be added and deleted.

The final selection is "Print Server Information." This allows you to add or delete print servers and to change their names. You must create a print server for each copy of PSERVER running on the network. For more information on print servers see Module 69.

APPLICATIONS

Use PCONSOLE for comprehensive control of print queues. Any user on the network has the need to display the current contents of a queue and to delete his own print jobs (if he should decide not to print them). Users also need to view available queue names and their corresponding printers. Only supervisors or queue operators, however, are allowed to delete anyone's jobs or make other changes to print queue information.

TYPICAL OPERATION

In this activity use PCONSOLE to view the total number of print jobs currently waiting in a queue. Begin at the DOS prompt of a logged-in workstation.

1. Type **PCONSOLE** and press **Enter**. Your screen shows:

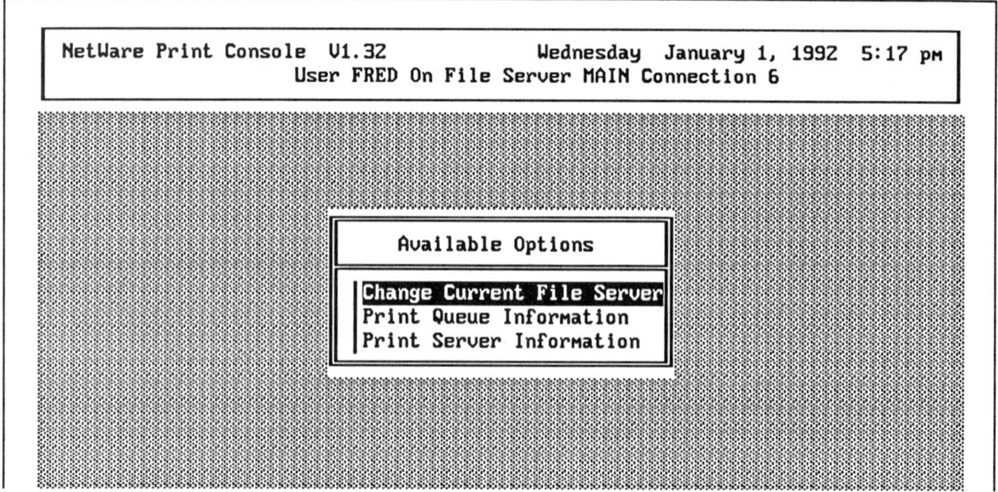

2. Use the **Up Arrow** and **Down Arrow** to highlight the second selection ("Print Queue Information") and press **Enter**.

3. Highlight any print queue name and press **Enter**. The screen now shows:

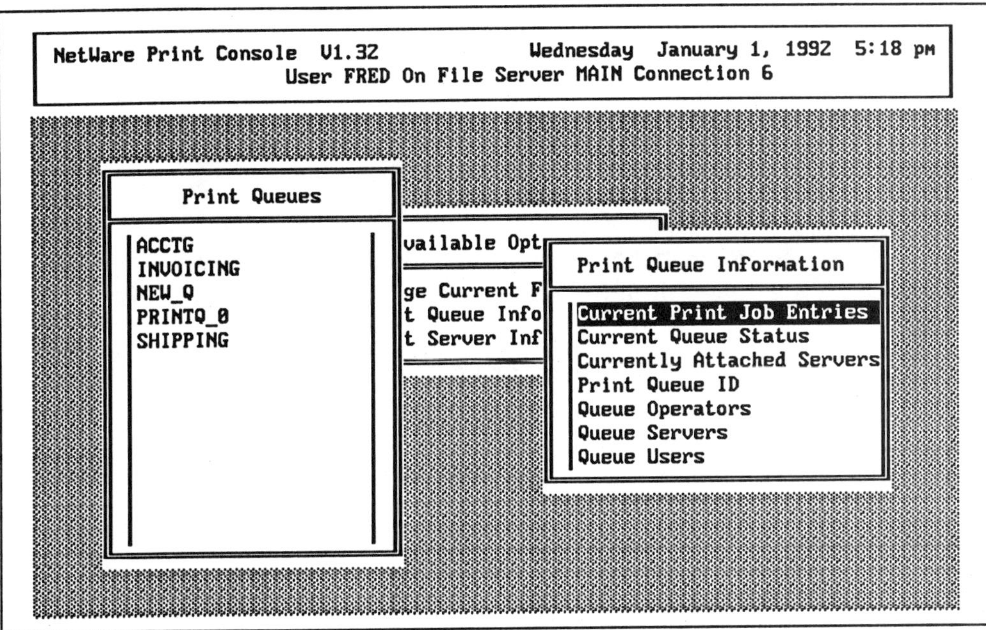

In this example, there are no print jobs waiting in this queue. Your screen may differ. Now exit PCONSOLE.

4. Press **Alt-F10**. The "Exit box" appears; press **Enter**.

5. Turn to Module 65 to continue the learning sequence.

Module 65
PRINTCON
(vers 2.x and 3.x)

DESCRIPTION

PRINTCON is a menu-driven utility. It allows the creation of custom print job configurations. The configurations you create are only available to your username, unless a supervisor copies them to another username. They can be used for printing files with NPRINT or CAPTURE (see modules 60 and 14).

When you type PRINTCON at a workstation prompt and press Enter, you see a menu similar to the following:

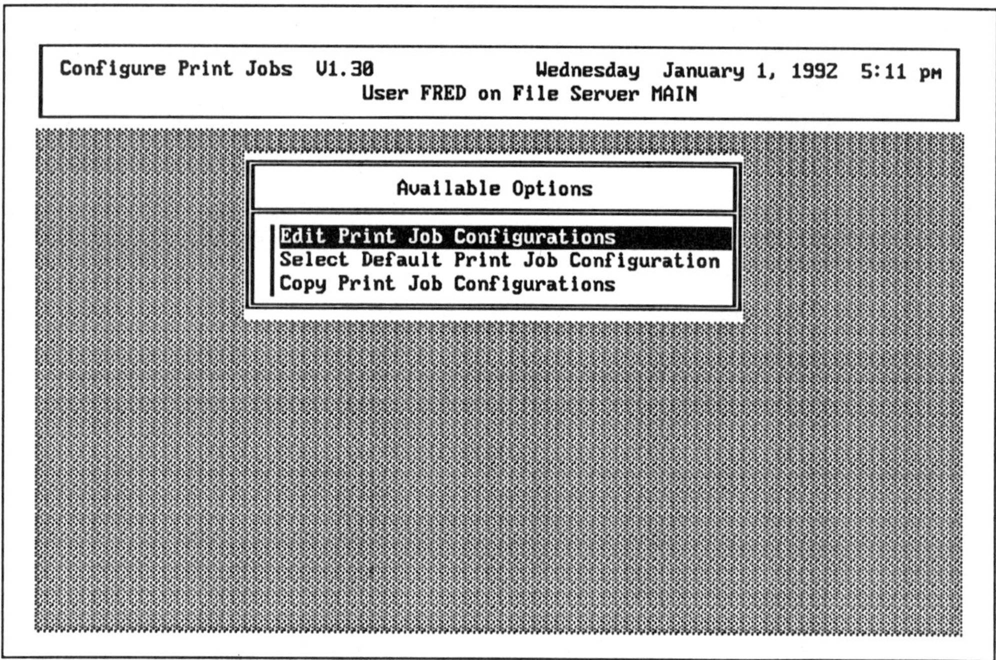

The main menu of this utility allows three options. The first, "Edit Print Job Configurations," is used to create, delete, and change print jobs. The second, "Select Default Print Job Configuration," lets you choose a print job (defined under menu option 1) to be the active one if no other job is selected when using NPRINT or CAPTURE. The last option, "Supervisor-Copy Print Job Configurations," allows a supervisor to copy one user's set of job configurations to another user. This also deletes any existing configurations for the target user. To exit PRINTCON you press Esc and type Y. You can also press Alt-F10 and type Y.

Many of the options that you can include in a job configuration are the same as the flags used with NPRINT and CAPTURE. The options and their purposes follow:

NUMBER OF COPIES	This option determines the number of copies to print. The default is 1.
SUPPRESS FORM FEED	This option lets you choose whether or not the printer will automatically issue form feeds. Most software will perform form feeds when necessary, therefore setting this option to NO may cause the printer to eject extra, blank pages. The default is to not suppress form feeds.
FILE CONTENTS	This option lets you identify the type of output being printed. TEXT is considered to be an ASCII file being copied directly to the print queue (typically with NPRINT). Special format characters, such as tabs, will be interpreted. The default is TEXT.
	Use BYTE STREAM when the output is coming from an application which is formatting it for the printer. In this case, *NetWare* assumes special characters are already interpreted.
TAB SIZE	This option is only valid when FILE CONTENTS is set to TEXT. Use it to tell *NetWare* how many spaces to insert when interpreting tab characters in the output. The default is 8.
FORM NAME	This option allows you to specify the type of form on which the file should be printed. Form names are defined in PRINTDEF (see Module 66). The default is to not use a predefined form name. Just before printing the file, the fileserver to which the target printer is attached verifies that the requested form is the same as the last one used on that printer. If not, a message is displayed asking that the appropriate form type be loaded. Once an operator has loaded the correct form, printing is resumed via the START PRINTER command at the fileserver console.
PRINT BANNER	This option lets you choose whether or not a banner page will be printed preceding your output. The default is YES.

BANNER NAME | This option lets you specify a username other than your own to be printed on the banner page. The default is your username.

BANNER FILE | This option lets you specify up to twelve characters to be printed on the banner page preceding the printout. The default is the name of the file being printed.

LOCAL PRINTER | This option, valid only with CAPTURE, is a single-digit number indicating the local parallel printer port (LPT1: through LPT3:) which is to be redirected by the CAPTURE command. The range is 1 to 3. The default is 1.

AUTO ENDCAP | This option is only valid with CAPTURE. It forces an ENDCAP (see Module 36) upon exiting an application. CAPTUREd or SPOOLed output is then transferred to the specified queue and printed. The default is Auto Endcap enabled.

ENABLE TIMEOUT | This option causes a spooled file to automatically close and transfer to the print queue a certain number of seconds after output has ceased. If you do not ENABLE TIMEOUT, many applications will require you to exit them before printing will commence. The default is TIMEOUT not ENABLED.

TIMEOUT COUNT | This option allows you to specify a number of seconds to wait after output to the spool file has ceased before issuing an automatic ENDCAP. The range is 0 to 1000. The option is meaningless unless you ENABLE TIMEOUT.

FILE SERVER | This option lets you select a fileserver from the available list as the target for the files to be printed. The server you choose does not have to be one to which you are currently logged or attached. *NetWare* will temporarily log in to that server, print the files, and log back out. This procedure uses the GUEST username. If a password has been assigned to GUEST, you are prompted to enter it. If the GUEST username has been deleted, you are given the opportunity to log in using any other valid username. The default is the fileserver to which you are currently logged.

PRINT QUEUE | This option allows the selection of the print queue you want to receive this print job. The default is the first queue on the specified printer. If no printer, fileserver, and queue are specified, the print job will be sent to the current default server, printer 0, and queue PRINTQ_0.

DEVICE

This option lets you select the device to which you print. The print queue selected must be assigned to this device.

MODE

This option lets you select a print mode for your print job. Typical print modes are condensed, letter quality, elite, etc. They are defined in PRINTDEF (see Module 66).

APPLICATIONS

PRINTCON is a key utility to *NetWare* printer services. It can be a tremendous time saver and encourages the use of more print options. Any commonly used configurations should be defined and given easy-to-remember names. The administrator may want to create job configurations common to most users, under a dummy username, and copy the set to new users.

TYPICAL OPERATION

In this activity you define a print job configuration. Begin at the DOS prompt of a logged-in workstation.

1. Type **PRINTCON** and press **Enter**. You see the PRINTCON menu, as illustrated in the beginning of this module.

2. Highlight the first option, using the Up and Down Arrow keys, and press **Enter**. You see a list of existing configurations.

   To change an existing configuration, you highlight it, and press Enter. To delete one, you highlight it and press Del. When asked to confirm the deletion, you highlight "Yes" and press Enter.

3. To create a new configuration, press **Ins**. Type **TESTCON** as a name for the configuration (it could be up to 31 characters), and press **Enter**.

4. Press **Alt-F10** to exit. Highlight "Yes" and press **Enter**.

5. Turn to Module 66 to continue the learning sequence.

Module 66
PRINTDEF
(ver 2.x and 3.x)

DESCRIPTION

PRINTDEF is a menu-driven utility which allows you to define print devices (printers and plotters) and print forms. These definitions can then be used when sending print jobs to network printers.

To define print devices, you need to provide control codes that are listed in the documentation that comes with the printer. There is a separate code for each function that the printer is capable of performing. These codes vary from printer to printer. Control codes usually start with the Esc character. Some have an obvious correlation to their purpose; the code to make an Epson FX286E printer print Emphasized is "Esc E." Many others are not so apparent; the code to make a Hewlett Packard Laserjet print in Underline is "Esc &dD."

After defining the print functions for a given print device, you can define print modes. A print mode is a combination of print functions that are called each time the mode is used. Suppose you want to define a mode to be used each time payroll checks are printed. You might include the functions "Reset" (to clear any previous functions), "LQ" (to put the printer in Letter Quality), and "10CPI" (to make the printer print 10 characters per inch). The function names, such as "LQ," are arbitrary. They are any descriptive term you wish to apply when defining print device functions.

PRINTDEF also allows you to define print forms. A print form is described, such as "3 Part NCR" or "Payroll Checks." It is then defined according to width and length. Each form definition has a unique number, within the 0-255 range.

After defining your devices and forms, you can refer to them each time you print a job. Both NPRINT and CAPTURE (modules 60 and 14) allow you to specify the print mode and form type to be used.

The menu of PRINTDEF offers these selections:

Print Devices

Edit Print Devices   This selection lists existing devices. You may use the Up Arrow and Down Arrow keys to select a device to change, or the Insert and Delete keys to create or delete devices.

PRINTDEF stores a list of functions for each device. Each function includes a descriptive name and the corresponding control codes. Edit this list as needed; use Esc to return to the main menu.

Device Modes

This option is available once print devices have been defined. Select a print device and select, create, or delete modes using the standard menu keys (see "Edit Print Devices" above). The mode "Reinitialize" will already exist and requires definition. Thereafter, create whatever other modes you need. To create a mode, assign it a descriptive name, and select the appropriate functions from the provided list.

Import Print Device

On multiserver networks, you can save time by copying print device definitions from one server to another. The first step in this process is to export the print device definition (see below). Now, ATTACH to the destination server, and reenter PRINTDEF. Select "Import Print Device" and enter the full path name to which you exported the definition. If a definition by the same name already exists on this server, you are prompted for a new name to be assigned.

Export Print Device

This is the first step in transferring a print device definition from one server to another. Select the device to export from the list of existing print devices. You are now prompted for a destination directory. Enter a valid complete path name. If you are exporting to a server named "ACCT," you can enter:

```
ACCT/SYS:PUBLIC
```

Now complete the process with Import Print Device, above.

Forms

You are given a list of existing forms. Select one to change, create, or delete using the standard menu keys. When creating a form, simply assign it a descriptive name, give it a form number (range 0 to 255), and define its length and width in lines and columns.

APPLICATIONS

PRINTDEF allows a great range of control over network printing. Normally, the administrator defines devices and forms and informs users of their proper use. Users can use PRINTDEF for reference to view available definitions.

TYPICAL OPERATION

In this activity use PRINTDEF to list the print device definitions available on your current fileserver. Begin at the DOS prompt of a logged-in workstation.

1. Type **PRINTDEF** and press **Enter**. The PRINTDEF main menu appears on your screen.

2. Select "Print Devices" using the Up Arrow and Down Arrow, and press **Enter**. Your screen shows:

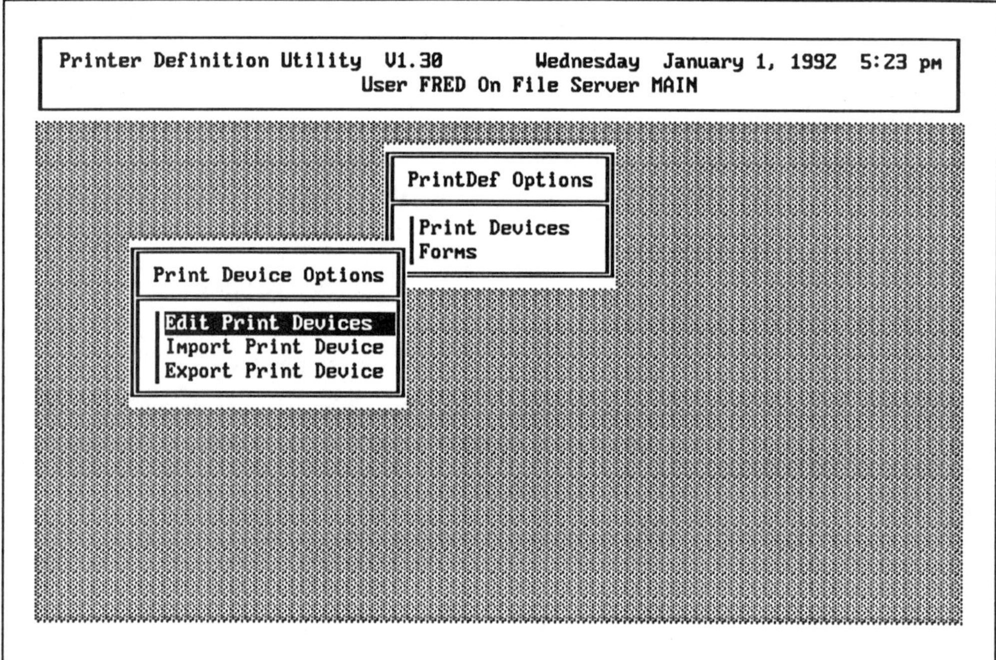

3. Select "Edit Print Devices" and press **Enter**. Your screen now lists any existing print device definitions.

4. Exit PRINTDEF by pressing **Alt-F10** and **Enter**.

5. Turn to Module 70 to continue the learning sequence.

Module 67
PRINTER
(ver 2.x)

DESCRIPTION

This module explains the use of 14 console commands that are related to network printing under *NetWare* 2.x. Many of these commands use the keyword "PRINTER."

These commands work with physical printers as well as print queues. A queue is a list of print jobs waiting to be printed. Jobs are held in the queue and sent to the appropriate printer one at a time in the order in which they are received. Queue commands allow you to change this order, delete waiting jobs, delete entire queues, or redirect a queue to a different printer. There is always one print queue for each network printer. You can create additional queues. Several queues may share one printer, and one queue may use several printers, passing jobs to each one as they are ready.

These are the console printer commands:

QUEUE RELATED COMMANDS

Add a Queue to a Printer

This command assigns an existing print queue to a network printer. The printer will service the queue, and any others that are currently assigned, according to the priority level of each queue. To add a queue called SALES to network printer 0, at the highest priority level, you use:

```
PRINTER 0 ADD QUEUE SALES AT PRIORITY 1
```

Change a Queue's Priority

This command changes the priority of a print job within an existing print queue. If you have a rush job and there are numerous jobs waiting in the queue before you, assign your job a higher priority. To do this, you must either be a supervisor, or a queue operator (see PCONSOLE, Module 64). To change a print job currently in the fifth position in a QUEUE named SALES to the first position, use:

```
QUEUE SALES CHANGE JOB 5 TO PRIORITY 1
```

Create a Queue

Use this command to create new queues that can then be assigned to network printers. To create a queue named SALES use:

```
QUEUE SALES CREATE
```

Delete a Job in a Queue

This command removes a single print job from a queue. To delete job 5 from queue SALES, use:

```
QUEUE SALES DELETE JOB 5
```

Delete All Jobs in a Queue

This command "flushes" a queue of all waiting print jobs. Use this with caution, as these jobs are completely deleted and will need to be recreated if users need them! To clear out a queue named sales, use:

```
QUEUE SALES DELETE
```

Delete a Queue

This command doesn't delete print jobs, but simply detaches the queue from a given printer. To remove queue SALES from printer 1, use:

```
PRINTER 1 DELETE QUEUE SALES
```

Destroy a Queue

This command deletes a queue and all jobs currently in it. Use this command with caution. To destroy queue SALES, use:

```
QUEUE SALES DESTROY
```

List Queues on a Printer

This command lists all queues currently attached to a given printer. To view queues attached to printer 1, use:

```
PRINTER 1 QUEUES
```

List All Queues

This command lists all queues and the printers to which they are currently attached. Simply use:

```
QUEUES
```

List a Queue's Jobs

This command lists all print jobs currently in a given queue. To list the jobs in queue SALES, use:

```
QUEUE SALES JOBS
```

PRINTER RELATED COMMANDS

Display a Printer's
Configuration

This command shows the configuration of the designated printer. For printer number 1:

    PRINTER 1 CONFIG

Set Printer Poll
Interval

This command determines how frequently *NetWare* checks print queues for new jobs. The default is 15 seconds. To set printer number 1 to 5 seconds:

    PRINTER 1 POLL 5

Rewind Printer

This useful command tells the print queue to back up a specified number of pages in the current print job and resume printing. This can save time when a long print job gets interrupted by printer problems, such as a paper jam. REWIND the printer 2-3 pages and resume. The printer should first be PAUSEd. If you don't specify the number of pages, the queue will back the job up to the beginning. To rewind printer number 2 up 5 pages:

    PRINTER 2 REWIND 5 PAGES

Stop Printer

This halts queue output to the printer. To Stop printer number 1:

    PRINTER 1 STOP

Start Printer

This resumes queue output to the printer. To Start printer number 1:

    PRINTER 1 START

FORM RELATED COMMANDS

Change Forms

This command tells *NetWare* that a new form type has been loaded into a network printer. Form types are defined with PRINTDEF (Module 66). After loading form 3 into printer 1, use:

    PRINTER 1 MOUNT FORM 3

Printer Form Feed

This command simply issues a form feed to the specified printer. The paper in that printer advances one page. For printer 1, use:

    PRINTER 1 FORM FEED

Mark Top of Form	This command tells *NetWare* that the paper in the specified printer is now aligned at a form break. For printer 1, use:

```
PRINTER 1 FORM MARK
```

OTHER COMMANDS

Printers	This command displays the current status of each network printer attached to this fileserver. The printer number, queues being serviced, form currently mounted, and On-Line/Off-Line status are included in the report. Simply use:

```
PRINTERS
```

APPLICATIONS

The PRINTER-related console commands provide the console operator a wide range of control over network printers. One of the great benefits in having a Novell network is the ability to spool printer output. With these commands the spooling procedure can be greatly enhanced.

TYPICAL OPERATION

In this activity you create a new print queue, list all print queues, and finally, destroy the queue. Begin at the DOS prompt of a logged-in workstation.

1. Type **QUEUE SALES CREATE** and press **Enter**.
2. Type **QUEUES** and press **Enter**. Note that the new queue, SALES, is listed along with any preexisting queues.
3. Type **QUEUE SALES DESTROY** and press **Enter**.
4. To verify the deletion of this queue, you can repeat step 2.
5. Turn to Module 61 to continue the learning sequence.

Module 68
PSC
(ver 3.x)

DESCRIPTION

PSC is a public command used to view certain information about Print Servers and network printers. Users that have been assigned Printer Server Operator status by a network administrator (through PCONSOLE, Module 64) can also use PSC to control print servers. There are 11 flags that are used with PSC. If you are not a Print Server Operator, you can only use the STATUS flag.

Flag	*Name*	*Description*
AB	ABORT	Deletes current print job, then proceeds to next (if any).
CD	CANCELDOWN	Cancels a DOWN request issued in PCONSOLE that would ordinarily DOWN the Print Server after the last jobs were printed.
FF	FORMFEED	Issues a Form Feed on the indicated printer. This printer must be PAUSEd or STOPped.
M	MARK	Allows you to align a printer by printing a row of asterisks at the current print position. You can follow the M flag with any other character to replace the *.
MO	MOUNT FORM	This flag is followed by the number of the next form to be mounted on the designated printer. Forms are defined using PRINTCON (Module 65). Whenever a print job requests a FORM number different than the last one MOUNTed, the print server stops and PAUSEs that printer until the MOUNT FORM flag is issued with PSC. Syntax is: MO = Form_number.

PAU	PAUSE	This flag temporarily PAUSEs the designated printer but keeps the current print job. When the printer is STARTed again, the print job resumes where it left off.
PRI	PRIVATE	This flag makes a printer only available locally (or to the workstation to which it is currently attached). It is no longer considered a network printer.
SH	SHARED	This flag negates the PRI flag. The printer is returned to network use.
STAT	STATUS	The STAT flag displays the current status of the designated printer. Any of the following messages might be reported:

In private mode
Mark/Form Feed
Mount form x
Not connected
Not installed
Off line
Out of paper
Paused
Printing job
Ready to go down
Stopped
Waiting for job

The syntax for PSC is:

```
PSC PS=Print_Server_Name P=Printer_Number Flags
```

Print_Server_Name is any valid Print Server. Use PCONSOLE (Module 64) to see which ones have been established. Printer_Number is the number assigned to that printer by the Print Server, once again defined in PCONSOLE.

APPLICATIONS

PSERVER allows you to attach network printers to any node that has been designated a Print Server (see Module 69). With PSC you can control these printers, no matter where they are on a network.

TYPICAL OPERATION

In this activity, display the current status of a printer number 0 attached to a Print Server named PS1. Begin at the workstation DOS prompt.

1. Type **PSC PS=PS1 P=0 STAT** and press **Enter**. The screen resembles this:

```
F:\>PSC PS=PS1 P=0 STAT
Usage: PSC PS[=]print_server P[=]printer_number FlagList ...
       FlagList:  CancelDown, FormFeed, PAUse,
                  PRIvate, SHared, STARt, STATus,
                  ABort,
                  STOp [Keep],
                  Mark [character], and
                  MOunt Form=n.

F:\>
```

2. Turn to Module 69 to continue the learning sequence.

Module 69
PSERVER
(ver 2.x and 3.x)

DESCRIPTION

PSERVER is a program that controls the distribution of print jobs. PSERVER moves print jobs that have been placed in the fileserver's queues to the appropriate printer. The printer can be attached to either a fileserver or a workstation. Some newer high-end printers have built-in network interfaces, allowing them to attach directly to the network cabling system.

A single PSERVER session controls up to 16 printers. PSERVER comes in three versions, each with a different file extension: VAP, NLM, and EXE. The VAP is loaded on a fileserver running the *NetWare* operating system version 2.x. The NLM is for fileservers running 3.x. The EXE is run on a dedicated workstation, meaning that when PSERVER is running no other task can be run. Typically, PSERVER.NLM or PSERVER.VAP is run at the fileserver. If more than 16 shared printers are needed on the network, PSERVER.EXE is run also. By having multiple dedicated workstations, a network can have a large number of shared printers. Some network administrators choose to only use the EXE version, relieving the fileserver of the overhead of running PSERVER.VAP or .NLM.

Regardless of the version of PSERVER, when the program is loaded you assign it a print server name as defined in PCONSOLE (Module 64). The VAP can be started and stopped using the commands "PSERVER START" and "PSERVER STOP" at the fileserver console. The VAP cannot however be unloaded. The NLM can be loaded and unloaded from the fileserver console. The EXE version cannot be unloaded. To do this the workstation must be reset.

Each workstation with printers attached that need to be shared must run a background program called RPRINTER. The user specifies which printers are to be shared and which queues and print server are to service them. PSC is a utility that allows you to control shared printers (Module 68).

APPLICATIONS

One of the most important reasons for having a local area network is the ability to share printers. PSERVER is part of a suite of *NetWare* software utilities which allow a comprehensive printer sharing environment. Use the PSERVER VAP or NLM (*NetWare* operating systems versions 2.x and 3.x, respectively) to provide shared printers to the network. Use PSERVER.EXE if you need to have more than 16 shared printers or to offload the PSERVER overhead from the fileserver.

TYPICAL OPERATION

In this activity, load the PSERVER NLM at a fileserver running 3.x. The print server is named PS1 and was created using PCONSOLE (Module 64). Begin at the fileserver console prompt.

1. Type **LOAD PSERVER PS1** and press **Enter**. The screen resembles this:

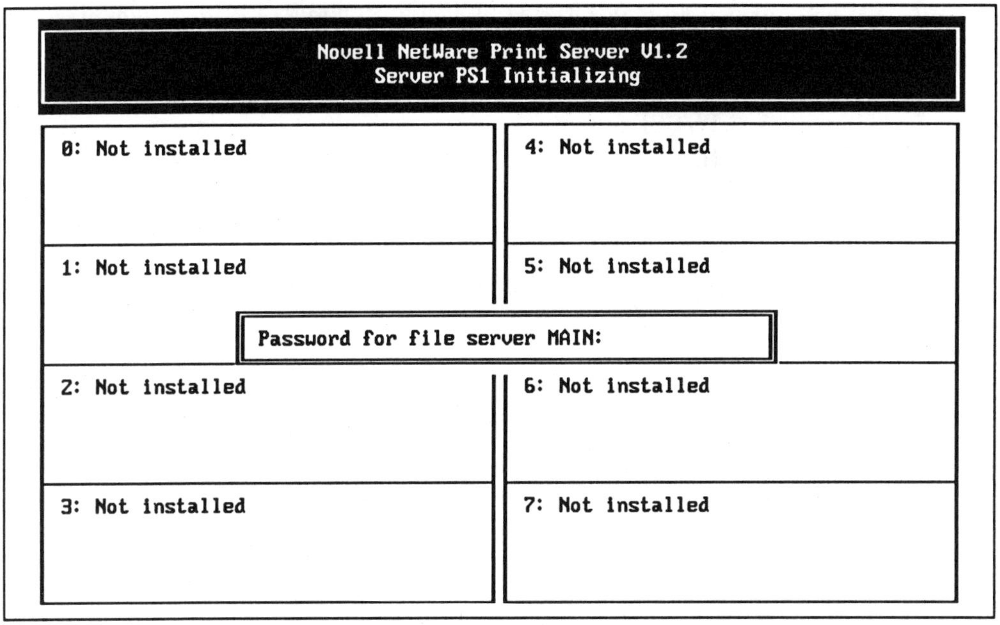

```
          Novell NetWare Print Server V1.2
               Server PS1 Initializing


0: Not installed                 4: Not installed



1: Not installed                 5: Not installed

        Password for file server MAIN:

2: Not installed                 6: Not installed



3: Not installed                 7: Not installed
```

2. Turn to Module 67 to continue the learning sequence.

Module 70
PSTAT
(ver 2.x)

DESCRIPTION

The public command PSTAT is used to display the status of network printers. Under *NetWare* 3.x, use PSC (Module 68) to accomplish this and other printer-related tasks. There are two flags which can follow PSTAT. Use the full name or the abbreviation.

S= (Server=) The parameter is any valid server name on the network. PSTAT reports on the printers attached to this server. If this flag is omitted, the current default server is assumed.

P= (Printer=) The parameter is a number 0-4. It determines the printer on the specified fileserver on which PSTAT will report. If this flag is omitted, PSTAT reports on all printers attached to the fileserver.

For each printer requested, PSTAT lists the on-line or off-line status, whether the printer is active or has been stopped (using the PRINTER console command, described in Module 67), and the form type currently loaded (as defined by PRINTDEF, Module 66).

APPLICATIONS

Use PSTAT to determine the status of network printers without having to leave your workstation. This is particularly helpful on networks with multiple shared printers. By listing the status of available printers prior to queueing print jobs (using NPRINT and CAPTURE modules 60 and 14), you can determine which printer is best suited to receive your work. If a certain printer is off-line (deselected or turned off at the printer) or stopped at the fileserver console, you may want to use a different printer. Also, if you need a particular form type, you can see if it is already loaded in a given printer.

TYPICAL OPERATION

In this activity you list the status of the first printer on the current default fileserver. Begin at the DOS prompt of a logged-in workstation.

1. Type **PSTAT P=0** and press **Enter**. The display resembles the following:

```
F:\INN>PSTAT P=0

Server MAIN: Network Printer Information
Printer     Ready      Status     Form: number, name
-------     ----------  ---------  ----------------------
   0        On-Line    Active      0, unknown name


F:\INN>
```

Next, report on all printers attached to a fileserver named ACCT.

2. Type **PSTAT S=ACCT** and press **Enter**. The display now shows:

```
F:\>PSTAT S=ACCTG

Server ACCTG: Network Printer Information
Printer     Ready      Status     Form: number, name
-------     ----------  ---------  ----------------------
   0        On-Line    Active      1, greenbar

   1        On-Line    Stopped     4, invoices

   3        Off-Line   Active      5, checks1


F:\>
```

3. Turn to Module 68 to continue the learning sequence.

Module 71
PURGE
(ver 2.x and 3.x)

DESCRIPTION

The public command PURGE forces the deletion of ERASEd files. The DOS ERASE (also called DEL) command appears to delete files, but actually they are only flagged for deletion. In both *NetWare* 2.x and *NetWare* 3.x PURGE has the effect of permanently removing such files. But there is a considerable difference in terms of how deleted files are managed.

Under 2.x the actual deletion does not occur until any command is executed from your workstation which creates or deletes other files, or until the PURGE command is issued. If you issue an ERASE (DEL) command which affects files that you did not want to delete, you can unERASE them by immediately using the SALVAGE command (see Module 77).

Under 3.x you can actually salvage files deleted days or even months ago! There are certain restrictions however. On a typical fileserver hard drive there is always storage space that is not being used. In fact it is wise to monitor drive storage and add or replace drives, or remove obsolete files, whenever drive capacity is over 80% full. *NetWare* 3.x takes advantage of whatever capacity is available (unused) on fileserver hard drives by using it to store deleted files. Only when there is no more room on a drive does it actually begin removing deleted files. For example, on a drive with a total capacity of 1 gigabyte which is only half full, *NetWare* will maintain the last 500 megabytes of deleted files. Any of these can be salvaged at any time! Depending on the nature of the files and applications in use, this could be a few days' worth of deletions or several months' worth.

As a result, the PURGE command can be of greater use under 3.x. When confidential files are erased, there is the risk of a security infringement if any user with the proper rights can salvage those files. Therefore, after erasing such files always issue a PURGE.

With either *NetWare* version, the PURGE command can be followed by a directory name and filename. The wild cards "*" and "?" are supported. If no directory or file names are specified, PURGE affects all deleted files in your current directory. There is one flag that can be used with PURGE. Ending the command with /ALL will purge files in the current directory, as well as any subdirectories.

APPLICATIONS

The PURGE command is used to permanently remove files which have been erased or deleted from fileserver hard drives.

TYPICAL OPERATION

In this activity you mark a file named TEST.NEW for deletion using the DOS ERASE command. Next, you complete the deletion process using PURGE. Start by creating TEST.NEW by using the DOS COPY command and the file TEST.TXT, created in Module 10. Begin at the DOS prompt of a logged-in workstation.

1. Type **CD\INN** and press **Enter**.
2. Type **COPY TEST.TXT TEST.NEW** and press **Enter**. The screen reports:

```
F:\INN>COPY TEST.TXT TEST.NEW
        1 file(s) copied

F:\INN>
```

3. Type **ERASE TEST.NEW** and press **Enter**.

At this point the file appears to be deleted. A directory listing will not include it. However, it could be restored using the SALVAGE command.

4. Type **PURGE TEST.NEW** and press **Enter**. The file is now permanently deleted. Depending on your *NetWare* version, your screen resembles one of the following:

```
F:\INN>ERASE TEST.NEW

F:\INN>PURGE TEST.NEW

TEST.NEW

Only specified files on MAIN
       have been purged from current directory.


F:\INN>
```

You can verify the PURGing of TEST.NEW using SALVAGE (Module 77).

5. Turn to Module 14 to continue the learning sequence.

Module 72
RCONSOLE
(ver 3.x)

DESCRIPTION

RCONSOLE is a *NetWare* utility that allows authorized users to monitor and control a fileserver from any attached workstation. To utilize RCONSOLE, two NLM programs must be loaded at the fileserver—REMOTE.NLM and RSPX.NLM. When REMOTE is loaded, a password is specified. Typically, this is to prevent anyone but network administrators from having access to fileservers.

The user runs RCONSOLE at the workstation. A list of all fileservers that have been set up for remote operation appears on the screen. With each fileserver selected, the correct password must be entered to gain access. At this point, the user's screen becomes a duplicate of the fileserver console. The entries at the console are mirrored at the workstation. Whatever is typed at the workstation appears at the fileserver. To end the session press Shift-Esc.

APPLICATIONS

While most of the administration of a Novell network is performed at the workstation, certain tasks require the administrator to type at the fileserver console. This can be quite inconvenient, especially in large networks where the fileserver and administrator's office may not even be on the same floor! Use RCONSOLE to instantly access, view, and control the fileserver console from anywhere on the network. This can help a single administrator manage even large, multiserver networks.

TYPICAL OPERATION

In this exercise prepare a fileserver for remote operation by loading RSPX and REMOTE. Assign the password "SUNSHINE." Then access the console from a workstation using RCONSOLE. Begin from the fileserver console prompt.

1. Type **LOAD REMOTE** and press **Enter**. You are now prompted for the password.

2. Type **SUNSHINE** and press **Enter**.

3. Now type **LOAD RSPX** and press **Enter**.

Next, go to your workstation. With the workstation logged in to the fileserver, begin at a DOS prompt.

4. Type **RCONSOLE** and press **Enter**. The screen resembles this:

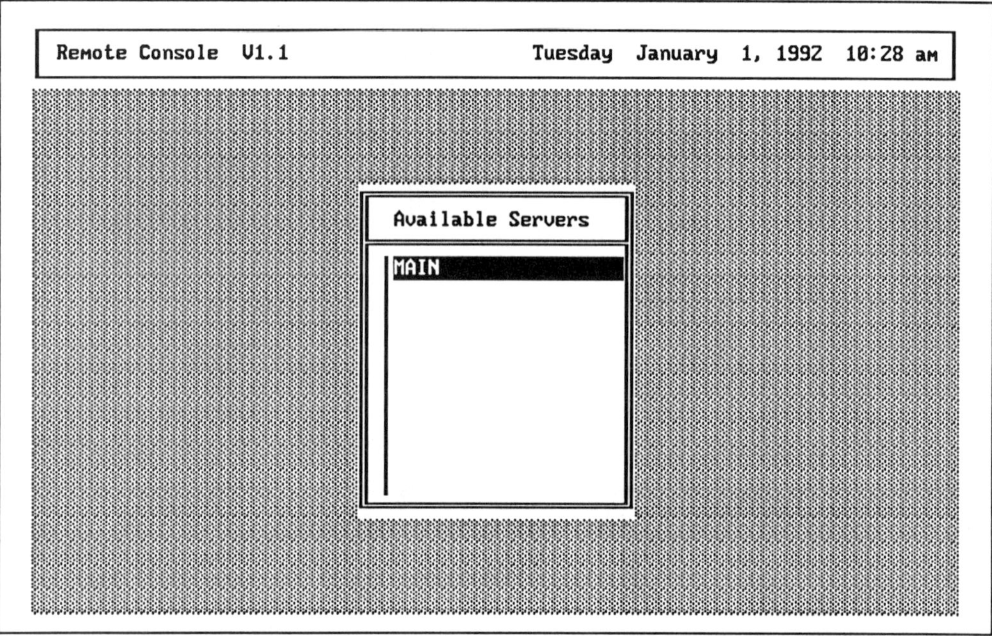

5. Use the arrow keys to highlight your fileserver, and press **Enter**. You are now prompted for a password.
6. Type **SUNSHINE** and press **Enter**.

At this time, whatever is on the fileserver console is reflected on your screen.

7. To exit RCONSOLE hold down the Shift key and press **Esc**.
8. Select YES and press **Enter**. You are now back to the RCONSOLE fileserver select screen.
9. Exit the screen by pressing **Esc**.
10. Turn to Module 37 to continue the learning sequence.

Module 73
REMOVE
(ver 2.x and 3.x)

DESCRIPTION

The public command REMOVE is used to remove any existing rights that a given user or group has within a directory. A user or group which is REMOVEd from a given directory is no longer considered a "trustee" of that directory. The command is followed by the name of the user or group and the directory name. The same action can be accomplished in a menu-driven environment using SYSCON (see Module 86). For more information on trustee rights, see GRANT (Module 41).

APPLICATIONS

REMOVE provides a quick, easy way to deny users all rights to a given directory. If the information kept in a directory becomes sensitive and requires increased security, existing trustees of that directory can be REMOVEd. Their rights can be later restored using the public command GRANT.

TYPICAL OPERATION

In this activity you REMOVE the user GUEST from being a trustee of the directory SYS:INN. GUEST is a username created by *NetWare* at the time of installation. You created SYS:INN in Module 10. Begin at the DOS prompt of a logged-in workstation.

1. Type **REMOVE GUEST FROM SYS:INN** and press **Enter**. The word "FROM" is optional. You are returned to a DOS prompt.

Verify the removal of GUEST from SYS:INN. Log in as GUEST and change to the \INN directory. Try viewing the files in that directory.

2. Type **LOGIN GUEST** and press **Enter**.

3. Type **CD\INN** and press **Enter**.

4. Type **DIR** and press **Enter**. Your display tells you "File not found."

5. Turn to Module 39 to continue the learning sequence.

Module 74
RENDIR
(ver 2.x and 3.x)

DESCRIPTION

RENDIR is used to rename a given directory. The command is followed by the old directory name, then the new name with the following syntax:

```
RENDIR current directory TO new name.
```

The word "TO" is optional. This ability is limited to users who have been assigned "parental" and "modify" rights to the directory which is to be changed. Such rights are assigned using RIGHTS or SYSCON, modules 76 and 86. Under *NetWare* 3.x, a directory cannot be renamed if it has been given the Rename inhibit attribute (see FLAGDIR, Module 40).

When a directory is renamed, whatever user rights had been assigned under the old directory name are maintained. Any drive mappings or other references to the old directory name (such as by a Menu) will have to be modified to reflect the new directory name.

APPLICATIONS

The naming of directories is important in maintaining a well-organized network volume. If a directory name no longer is descriptive of its purpose or if the creation of a new directory causes conflict with an existing directory name, use RENDIR to change the name. Remember that other users (as well as the LOGIN SCRIPTS, Module 50) may be expecting the old directory name. Be sure to inform users of such changes as appropriate.

TYPICAL OPERATION

In this activity you create a subdirectory called SYS:INN\APPLE. Then change the name of the directory to SYS:INN\ORANGE. The SYS:INN directory was created in Module 8. Begin at the DOS prompt of a logged-in workstation.

1. Type **CD\INN** and press **Enter**. Next type **MD APPLE** and press **Enter**. These are standard DOS commands. To verify the creation of the directory, type **DIR** and press **Enter**. Your display shows:

```
F:\INN>MD APPLE

F:\INN>DIR

 Volume in drive F is SYS
 Volume Serial Number is 9901-7CD9
 Directory of F:\INN

321        EXE         16 01-01-91    1:31p
TEST       TXT         16 01-01-92    5:39p
TEST       PRN         16 01-01-92    1:49p
PRACTICE      <DIR>       02-05-92   12:59p
APPLE         <DIR>       02-05-92    6:11p
        5 file(s)           48 bytes
                      8568832 bytes free

F:\INN>
```

2. Type **RENDIR APPLE TO ORANGE** and press **Enter**. The word "TO" is optional. You now see:

```
F:\INN>RENDIR APPLE TO ORANGE
Directory renamed to ORANGE

F:\INN>
```

3. Turn to Module 52 to continue the learning sequence.

Module 75
REVOKE
(ver 2.x and 3.x)

DESCRIPTION

The public command REVOKE is used to remove certain rights that a given user (or group) may have for a given directory. *NetWare* 3.x also allows rights to be GRANTed or REVOKEd for individual files.

It is similar to REMOVE (see Module 73) except that it allows you to REVOKE only the rights you select. These rights are assigned using the PUBLIC command GRANT (see Module 41). They can also be assigned or revoked in a menu-driven environment using SYSCON (see Module 86). You follow the command by the initials of the rights to be REVOKEd, the directory name, and the user or group name in this format:

REVOKE xxx FOR directory name FROM username

There are seven basic rights for both 2.x and 3.x:

Right	*Description*
READ	Open file and read contents.
WRITE	Open file and write to it.
CREATE	Create new files and directories.
ERASE	Delete files and directories.
MODIFY	Change file or directory name or attributes.
FILE SCAN	See files (but not necessarily open them).
ACCESS CONTROL	Grant file or directory rights to other users.

There is one right unique to 3.x:

SUPERVISORY	This grants all rights and overrides any other restrictions that have been placed on this user within this directory structure.

You can also use the keyword ALL, to specify all rights. Using REVOKE ALL has the same effect as the REMOVE command.

APPLICATIONS

REVOKE provides a quick, easy way to deny users certain rights to a given directory. If the information kept in a directory becomes sensitive and requires increased security, you may wish to deny some rights from other users. Their rights can be later restored using the public command GRANT (see Module 41).

TYPICAL OPERATION

In this activity you REVOKE the user GUEST's right to read files in the SYS:INN directory. GUEST is a username created by *NetWare* during installation. You created SYS:INN in Module 10. Begin at the DOS prompt of a logged-in workstation.

1. Type **REVOKE R FOR \INN FROM GUEST** and press **Enter**. The word "FROM" is optional. You are returned to a DOS prompt.

Verify that the right to read files in the SYS:INN directory has been REVOKEd. Log in as GUEST. Then change to the \INN directory and try to read a file.

2. Type **LOGIN GUEST** and press **Enter**.

3. Type **CD\INN** and press **Enter**.

4. Type **DIR** and press **Enter**. No files will be listed on the screen.

5. Turn to Module 73 to continue the learning sequence.

Module 76
RIGHTS
(ver 2.x and 3.x)

DESCRIPTION

A listing of the rights or privileges that you have been assigned in a given directory is obtained using the public command RIGHTS. This can also be done in a menu-driven environment using the SYSCON utility (see Module 86). To specify a directory, follow the command with a backslash and the complete directory path, or its path relative to your current directory. Omit the directory name to view your rights in the current default directory.

These rights may include:

Right	Description
READ	Open file and read contents.
WRITE	Open file and write to it.
CREATE	Create new files and directories.
ERASE	Delete files and directories.
MODIFY	Change file or directory name or attributes.
FILE SCAN	See files (but not necessarily open them).
ACCESS CONTROL	Grant file or directory rights to other users.
SUPERVISORY	(*NetWare* 3.x only) This grants all rights, and overrides any other restrictions that have been placed on this user within this directory structure.

They are assigned and modified using the SYSCON utility or through GRANT (see Module 41).

APPLICATIONS

Use RIGHTS to determine what file privileges you have in a given directory.

TYPICAL OPERATION

In this activity you list your assigned rights for the current directory. Begin at the DOS prompt of a logged-in workstation.

1. Type **RIGHTS** and press **Enter**. The screen should resemble this:

```
F:\>RIGHTS
MAIN\SYS:
Your Effective Rights for this directory are [SRWCEMFA]
      You have Supervisor Rights to Directory.     (S)
    * May Read from File.                          (R)
    * May Write to File.                           (W)
      May Create Subdirectories and Files.         (C)
      May Erase Directory.                         (E)
      May Modify Directory.                        (M)
      May Scan for Files.                          (F)
      May Change Access Control.                   (A)

  * Has no effect on directory.

      Entries in Directory May Inherit [SRWCEMFA] rights.
      You have ALL RIGHTS to Directory Entry.

  F:\>
```

Now check your rights for a different directory — \PUBLIC.

2. Type **RIGHTS \PUBLIC** and press **Enter**. Note the display:

```
F:\>RIGHTS \PUBLIC
MAIN\SYS:PUBLIC
Your Effective Rights for this directory are [SRWCEMFA]
      You have Supervisor Rights to Directory.     (S)
    * May Read from File.                          (R)
    * May Write to File.                           (W)
      May Create Subdirectories and Files.         (C)
      May Erase Directory.                         (E)
      May Modify Directory.                        (M)
      May Scan for Files.                          (F)
      May Change Access Control.                   (A)

  * Has no effect on directory.

      Entries in Directory May Inherit [SRWCEMFA] rights.
      You have ALL RIGHTS to Directory Entry.

  F:\>
```

3. Turn to Module 41 to continue the learning sequence.

Module 77
SALVAGE
(ver 2.x and 3.x)

DESCRIPTION

The public menu-driven utility SALVAGE "unerases" files which have not yet been permanently deleted. The DOS ERASE (also called DEL) command appears to delete files, but actually they are only marked for deletion and can be restored using the SALVAGE command. While salvage is used in both *NetWare* 2.x and 3.x, the commands and their capabilities differ considerably. This is because of the different ways that each version manages deleted files.

Under 2.x the actual deletion does not occur until a command is executed from your workstation which creates or deletes other files, or until the PURGE command is issued. If you issue an ERASE (DEL) command which affects files that you did not want to delete, you can unERASE them by immediately using the SALVAGE command.

Under 3.x you can actually salvage files deleted days or even months ago! There are certain restrictions, however. On a typical fileserver hard drive there is always storage space that is not being used. In fact it is wise to monitor drive storage and add or replace drives, or remove obsolete files, whenever drive capacity is over 80% full. *NetWare* 3.x takes advantage of whatever capacity is available (unused) on fileserver hard drives by using it to store deleted files. Only when there is no more room on a drive does it actually begin removing deleted files. For example, on a drive with a total capacity of 1 gigabyte which is only half full, *NetWare* will maintain the last 500 megabytes of deleted files. Any of these can be salvaged at any time! Depending on the nature of the files and applications in use, this could be a few days' worth of deletions or several months' worth.

Upon entering the 2.x SALVAGE utility, there are two selections. The first allows you to select the volume and directory from which to salvage files. The second begins the salvage process. Deleted (but not purged) files are listed, and you select which ones to restore.

The 3.x SALVAGE utility has more options. The first is to select a directory which has been deleted. This would not be possible under 2.x, as the deleted files would be purged upon issuing the command to delete the directory. The second option is to select a nondeleted directory. The third allows you to determine how salvage files will be sorted, when listed by the fourth option. Choices for sorting include deletion date, file size, file name (alphabetically), and owner's name (whoever created the file). The fourth option lists deleted files accordingly and allows you to select which ones to restore. Remember, *NetWare* 3.x retains as many deleted files as it has room for. As newer files are deleted, *NetWare* makes room to retain them by purging older files.

APPLICATIONS

Under *NetWare* 2.x use SALVAGE to restore files that have just been accidentally ERASEd. Under 3.x use SALVAGE to also restore files which *NetWare* has not yet been forced to purge due to disk space limitations, and which no user has yet chosen to purge.

TYPICAL OPERATION

In this activity you ERASE a file named TEST.TXT, then restore it using SALVAGE. TEST.TXT is located in the default directory. The screens below are from *NetWare* 2.1. Begin at the DOS prompt of a logged-in workstation.

1. Type **ERASE TEST.TXT** and press **Enter**.

CAUTION

At this point if you issue the PURGE command or if you perform any operation that creates, deletes, or erases other files, the TEST.TXT will be permanently lost.

2. Type **SALVAGE** and press **Enter**. Notice the display:

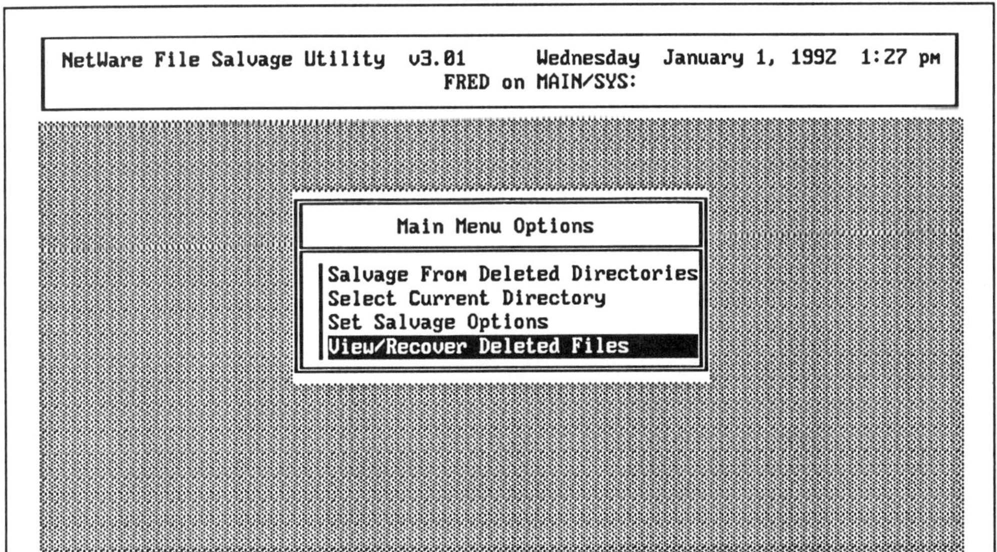

3. Select **SALVAGE FILES** and press **Enter**.

4. Select the TEST.TXT file and press **Enter**.

5. Use the **Esc** key to exit this utility.

6. Turn to Module 71 to continue the learning sequence.

Module 78
SECURITY
(ver 2.x and 3.x)

DESCRIPTION

SECURITY is a seemingly "intelligent" system command that analyzes the network for potential weak points in security. These include:

- Allowing users to have no password, short passwords (less than five characters), or passwords that are the same as the username.
- Allowing users to have rights in the root directory (and thus possible rights in all other directories), or more than the default rights in the \SYSTEM, \PUBLIC, and other *NetWare* system directories.
- Allowing users to have "supervisor" status and thus full access to all resources of the network.

SECURITY checks for such occurrences and reports them on your workstation display. You can obtain a hard copy of the SECURITY findings by using the DOS "> PRN" to redirect screen output to a printer.

APPLICATIONS

NetWare is capable of very sophisticated security configurations but there are a number of oversights an administrator may make in maintaining the system. Therefore, it is important to periodically run SECURITY and correct any reported problems as you see fit.

TYPICAL OPERATION

In this activity you print a report of potential network security breaks. Begin at the DOS prompt of a logged-in workstation.

1. To send the report to a local printer, ensure that the local printer port is not redirected to the network—type **ENDCAP** and press **Enter**. To direct the report to a network printer (in this case Queue LASER on the default server), type **CAPTURE Q=LASER** and press **Enter**. ENDCAP and CAPTURE are covered in modules 36 and 14.
2. Type **SECURITY > PRN** and press **Enter**.
3. Turn to Module 11 to continue the learning sequence.

Module 79
SEND
(ver 2.x and 3.x)

DESCRIPTION

The public command SEND transmits messages immediately to other users. The messages can be from one to 40 characters and must always be enclosed in quotes. The message is displayed on the 25th (bottom) line of the designated user's screen. The menu-driven utility SESSION (Module 80) also allows the sending of messages.

You can specify one or more users to receive a single message, or use any existing group name. If the recipient is not logged in to the default fileserver, you must precede their username by their fileserver name and a forward slash. You can use a wild card (*) to represent all fileservers to which you are attached. If you attempt to SEND a message to a nonexistent user or one who has not logged in, you receive an appropriate message concerning that situation. A user's current station number can be substituted for a username. A list of logged-in users and their current station numbers can be obtained via the USERLIST command. Finally, *console* can be specified as a username to send messages to fileservers.

To clear a message which you receive, press Ctrl-Enter.

APPLICATIONS

SEND is a very useful command and should ideally be learned by all users. It can greatly enhance interoffice communication as well as streamline the job of the network administrator.

TYPICAL OPERATION

In this activity you use the SEND command to transmit several messages. The first message is to a user named Fred who is logged in to the ACCT fileserver. Begin at the DOS prompt of a logged-in workstation.

1. Type **SEND "Have the income statement finished by noon" to ACCT/FRED**, and press **Enter**. Your screen resembles this:

```
F:\>SEND "HAVE THE INCOME STATEMENT FINISHED BY NOON" TO ACCTG/FRED
Message sent to ACCTG/FRED (station 4).

F:\>
```

In the following step, you SEND a message to both Bob and Fred. They are logged in to the default fileserver.

2. Type **SEND "Come to my office at once!" to FRED, BOB** and press **Enter**.

Next, SEND a message to everyone on the default fileserver.

3. Type **SEND "Log out by 5:00" to EVERYONE** and press **Enter**.

SEND the next message to all users on all attached fileservers.

4. Type **SEND "Log out by 5:00" to */EVERYONE** and press **Enter**.

Finally, SEND a message to the fileserver.

5. Type **SEND "Change printer 1 to font cartridge B" to CONSOLE** and press **Enter**.

6. Turn to Module 15 to continue the learning sequence.

Module 80
SESSION
(ver 2.x and 3.x)

DESCRIPTION

SESSION is a menu-driven utility used to interface with *NetWare* and modify the user's environment without causing any changes that will last beyond the current session. In other words, any configuration changes made with SESSION are temporary and cease to exist after logging out. Therefore, SESSION is a suitable utility for all users. SESSION includes the following options:

Change Current Server	This lists available fileservers and allows you to select the one which will be your default. You can LOGIN (Module 48) to a new server or under a new username.
Drive Mappings	This allows you to view and change the current drive mappings (see MAP, Module 52).
Group List	This allows you to view groups and send them messages.
Search Mappings	This allows you to view and change search mappings (once again, refer to MAP, Module 52).
Select Default Drive	This lets you determine which drive will be your current default drive.
User List	This is similar to the public command USERLIST (Module 90). It provides a list of all current users. You can select any user and view information concerning them or send them a message.

As with all menu-driven utilities, use the Up and Down Arrow keys to make your selections. The Esc key moves you back through the menus. Press Alt-F10 and Y to exit.

APPLICATIONS

SESSION allows users to change drive mappings, select default drives, attach to fileservers, and send messages, all from within a user-friendly menu-driven environment. Many users may not want to learn and remember such commands as MAP, ATTACH, and SEND.They will find it easier to use SESSION.

TYPICAL OPERATION

In this activity you use two of the options available within SESSION. Begin at the DOS prompt of a logged-in workstation.

1. Type **SESSION** and press **Enter**. The screen resembles this:

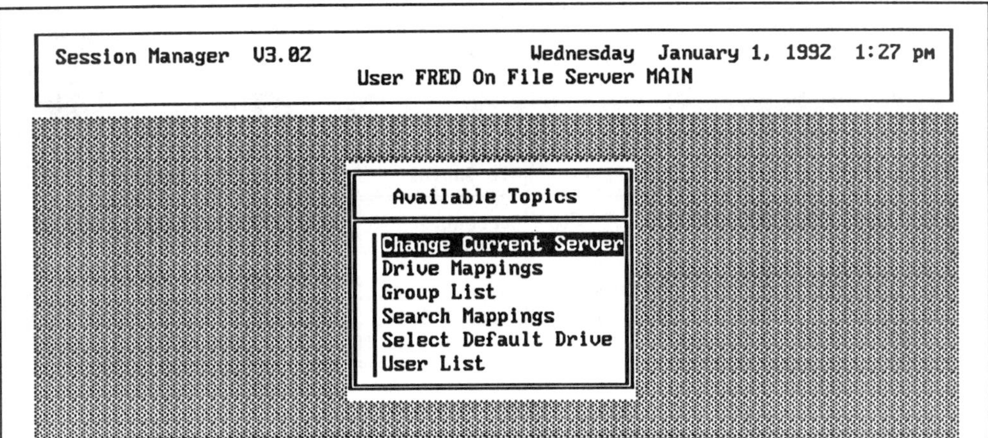

2. Press **Enter** to select the first option, Change Current Server. By selecting this option, you are actually performing the public command ATTACH. Since it is assumed that you only have one fileserver to which you may be attached, only the name of your fileserver will be shown in the box, as is shown here:

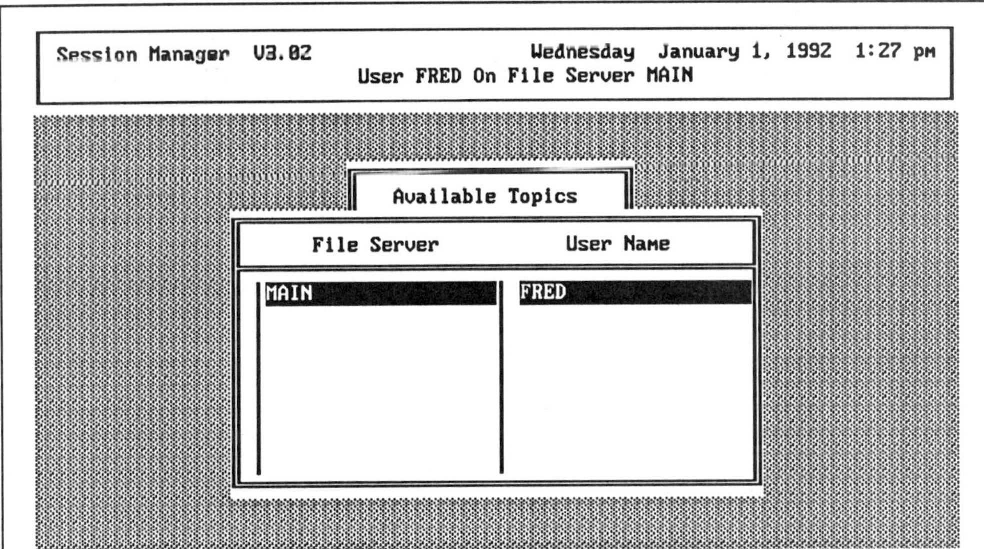

3. Press **Esc** to back up to the Available Options Menu.

4. Press the **Down Arrow** to select User List and press **Enter**. This selection is the same as typing USERLIST at the workstation's DOS prompt. The screen resembles the following:

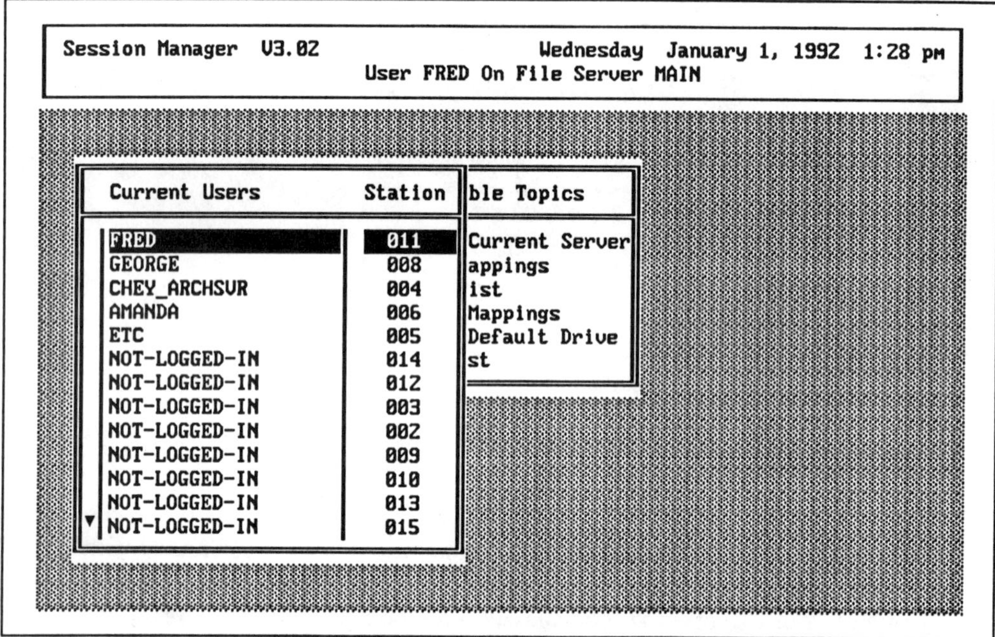

5. Press **Esc** to again back up to the Available Options Menu.

6. To exit SESSION press **Alt-F10**. Highlight "Yes" and press **Enter**.

7. Turn to Module 38 to continue the learning sequence.

Module 81
SETPASS
(ver 2.x and 3.x)

DESCRIPTION

SETPASS is a public command which allows you to assign or exchange the password associated with your username. This can also be accomplished in a menu-driven environment using the SYSCON utility (see Module 86). To change your password on a fileserver other than the default, you can follow the SETPASS command with a valid fileserver name. Passwords are up to 127 characters and can combine alpha and numeric characters. They cannot include control characters.

APPLICATIONS

To quickly create or change your password, use SETPASS.

TYPICAL OPERATION

In this activity you assign the password "SUNSHINE" to your username on the current default fileserver. Begin at the F>.

1. Type **SETPASS** and press **Enter**. Note the display:

```
F:\>SETPASS
Changing password for MAIN/FRED
Enter your old password:
```

2. Type your old password and press **Enter**. If you are assigning your password for the first time, press **Enter**. The screen responds:

```
F:\>SETPASS
Changing password for MAIN/FRED
Enter your old password:
Enter your new password:
```

3. Type **SUNSHINE** and press **Enter**. The characters are not displayed as you type them. *NetWare* does not distinguish between uppercase and lowercase. You are now asked to verify:

```
F:\>SETPASS
Changing password for MAIN/FRED
Enter your old password:
Enter your new password:
Retype your new password:
```

4. Once more, type **SUNSHINE** and press **Enter**. Be careful to remember your new password. Note the display:

```
F:\>SETPASS
Changing password for MAIN/FRED
Enter your old password:
Enter your new password:
Retype your new password:
Your password has been changed.

F:\>
```

5. Turn to Module 84 to continue the learning sequence.

Module 82
SET TIME
(ver 2.x and 3.x)

DESCRIPTION

You use the console command SET TIME to change the fileserver's clock to the actual date and time. You follow the command by the correct date and/or time, separated by a space. It is not necessary to specify both the time and date if one of them is already correct. Enter the time in the form HOUR:MINUTE:SECOND. Seconds can be omitted. The hour is a number 0-23, starting and ending at midnight. In other words, 10:30 A.M. is entered 10:30:00; and 10:30 P.M. is entered 22:30:00. Enter the date as MM/DD/YY.

APPLICATIONS

Use SET TIME to correct an invalid date and/or time when a fileserver is booted (see Module 8). If the fileserver is always on or has a battery powered clock, the date and time should be automatically maintained (even in leap years). Daylight Savings Time, however, is not accounted for and will require adjusting the time with SET TIME.

TYPICAL OPERATION

In this activity you change the fileserver's date and time to 03/27/91 and 15:15:00 (3:15 P.M.) then change it back to the current date and time. Begin at the : prompt of your fileserver.

1. Type **SET TIME 03/27/91 15:15:00** and press **Enter**. Now, use the TIME command (see Module 88) to verify that the change has occurred.

2. Type **TIME** and press **Enter**. The display shows the time that you entered in step 1.

3. Type **SET TIME**, followed by today's date and the correct time, and press **Enter**. Be sure to use the TIME command to verify the correct time and date.

4. Turn to Module 23 to continue the learning sequence.

Module 83
SHOWFILE
(ver 2.x and 3.x)

DESCRIPTION

SHOWFILE is a system command which cancels the effects of HIDEFILE (see Module 46). SHOWFILE restores the ability to list specified files and to delete or copy over them.

You follow the command with the name of the file to show. You can precede the filename with its path (drive specification and directory name) if different from the current path. You can also use wild cards (* and ?) in specifying the filename(s).

APPLICATIONS

To make files which were previously hidden and protected by HIDEFILE available to all users, use SHOWFILE.

TYPICAL OPERATION

In this activity you remove the hidden and protected status of a file named "TEST.TXT" which was hidden in Module 46. Begin at the DOS prompt of a logged-in workstation.

1. Type **SHOWFILE TEST.TXT** and press **Enter**. The screen resembles this:

```
F:\INN>SHOWFILE TEST.TXT
MAIN/SYS:INN
      TEST.TXT          visible

F:\INN>
```

2. Turn to Module 45 to continue the learning sequence.

Module 84
SLIST
(ver 2.x and 3.x)

DESCRIPTION

The public command SLIST lists all active fileservers attached to your default server. Fileservers which are not currently on-line are not listed. Included in the fileserver listing is the name of the network on which each fileserver resides, as well as the node address (a unique hexadecimal number assigned to each NIC). On single fileserver networks the SLIST command is of little importance. The following flag can be used with SLIST.

C (Continuous)   This flag causes the information reported by SLIST to scroll continuously on your screen. Otherwise, you must press a key to continue after every screenfull.

APPLICATIONS

On a network with more than one server, use SLIST to determine what fileservers are available to you.

TYPICAL OPERATION

In this activity you list all operational fileservers physically attached to your default server. Begin at the DOS prompt of a logged-in workstation.

1. Type **SLIST** and press **Enter**. A list of known servers and the node addresses is displayed:

```
F:\INN>SLIST
Known NetWare File Servers              Network    Node Address
---------------------------             --------   --------------
ACCTG                                   [     1] [        FA3D] Attached
MAIN                                    [    33] [           1] Default

Total of 2 file servers found

F:\INN>
```

2. Turn to Module 10 to continue the learning sequence.

Module 85
SMODE
(ver 2.x and 3.x)

DESCRIPTION

The public command SMODE determines the way in which specified executable files search for data files. Most applications require access to data files. Under DOS, data files are either located in the same directory as the application, or the application is written to look for data in other specific directories. *NetWare* can limit these two options or provide the application the ability to search for data stored in other directories. These alternate search directories are established using the MAP command, either as a public command (see Module 52) or in login scripts (see Module 50). There are 6 ways to search:

0	This is the default. It tells *NetWare* to follow search modes established in the SHELL.CFG file (see Module 7).
1	In this mode, applications will search only in directories as determined in the program. If none are specified in the program, *NetWare* will search the current default directory, and finally the search paths defined by MAP.
2	In this mode the application only searches the current default directory.
3	This mode is the same as mode 1, except that any directories not specified in the program can only be opened "read-only."
4	There is no mode number 4.
5	This mode is like mode 1, except that if the needed data files are not found in the directory specified in the program, *NetWare* continues its search—first in the default directory, then in the search paths defined by MAP.
6	There is no mode number 6.
7	In this mode applications may search directories specified in the program, the default directory, and the search paths, as long as the data files are opened "read-only."

Modes 4 and 6 are reserved.

The SMODE command is followed by the path (if different than the current default) and the filename of the program, then the mode number. The typical syntax is:

SMODE *fileserver name/volume name:directory name\filemask mode*

If any of the information is omitted, the default is assumed. If a mode is not specified, the current SMODE status is displayed.

APPLICATIONS

SMODE is used both to expand and to limit the way in which applications search for data. You may have an application whose data you wish to keep in different directories. If the application does not allow you to tell it where to look for data files, mode 5 will allow it any search paths established by the MAP command. On the other hand, it is possible that different applications may use data files of the same name. It is important that your program not read the files of others. Use mode 2 to limit access to data files in the current default directory.

TYPICAL OPERATION

In this activity you restrict any program with an EXE or COM extension from accessing data files located outside that directory. Begin at the DOS prompt of a logged-in workstation. In this example use a file called MAIN.EXE.

1. Type **SMODE MAIN.EXE 2** and press **Enter**. The display shows:

```
F:\INN>SMODE MAIN.EXE 2
MAIN/SYS:INN
   MAIN.EXE      Mode = 2, do not search

F:\INN>
```

2. Turn to Module 58 to continue the learning sequence.

Module 86
SYSCON
(ver 2.x and 3.x)

DESCRIPTION

SYSCON is a menu-driven utility you use to establish, monitor, and alter system configuration information in a number of different ways. This includes fileserver, accounting, group, workgroup, user, login script, AUTOEXEC.NCF (with 3.x), and other information. The SYSCON menu looks like this:

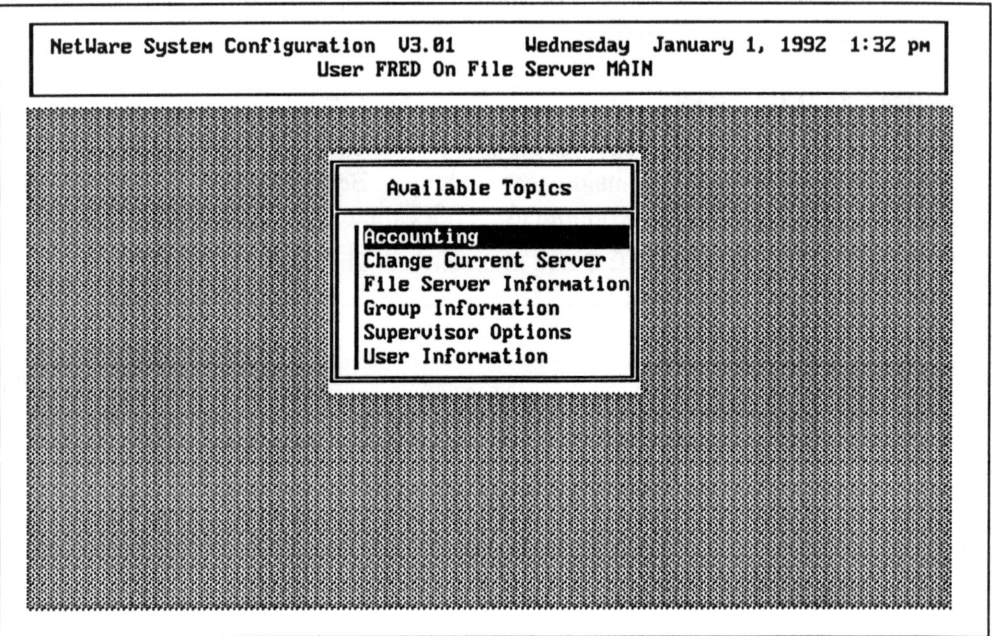

Certain menu selections are available only to users with supervisor privileges. The options from the opening menu of SYSCON and their purpose are as follows.

Menu Selection	Purpose
Accounting	Track use of the network by each user to determine use patterns and billing levels.
Change Current Server	Select a different fileserver to be configured by SYSCON.
File Server Information	Various information about the type and configuration of fileservers.
Group Information	Create, define, and display user groups.
Supervisor Options	Monitor accounting and login restrictions, define autoexec and login script files, list fileserver errors.
User Information	Create, define, and display user information (rights, restrictions, passwords, etc.). Also create, define, and display work group members and managers.

APPLICATIONS

While the SYSCON utility is often used by all users on a network, it is most extensively used by network administrators. On newly installed networks, SYSCON allows you to define users and user groups. This includes establishing which files and directories can be accessed by each user or group of users, and in what way they can be affected. You can also establish the days and times during which given users can log in, passwords for each user, and other security-related information.

Login scripts are defined with the SYSCON utility. These are a set of instructions executed each time a user logs in to a fileserver. The instructions establish drive mappings, search paths, the location of the DOS command processor (command.com), and other important information. When a user logs in, an individual login script is executed (if one exists), followed by a system login script (if any) that applies to all users.

SYSCON also allows you to create and maintain a network accounting system. Network accounting tracks use of the fileserver(s) by each user based on time logged in and out, number of requests, amount of data written and read, printer access, and amount of disk storage used. This information is then used to determine a scheme to bill individual users or departments within a company for overall network use.

TYPICAL OPERATION

In this activity you use SYSCON to view information about the fileserver. Begin at the DOS prompt of a logged-in workstation.

1. Type **SYSCON** and press **Enter**.

2. Highlight File Server Information using the Arrow keys. Press **Enter**.

A list of available fileservers is displayed. On single server networks, of course, there is only one choice.

3. Highlight one of the fileservers listed and press **Enter**. Your screen now resembles this:

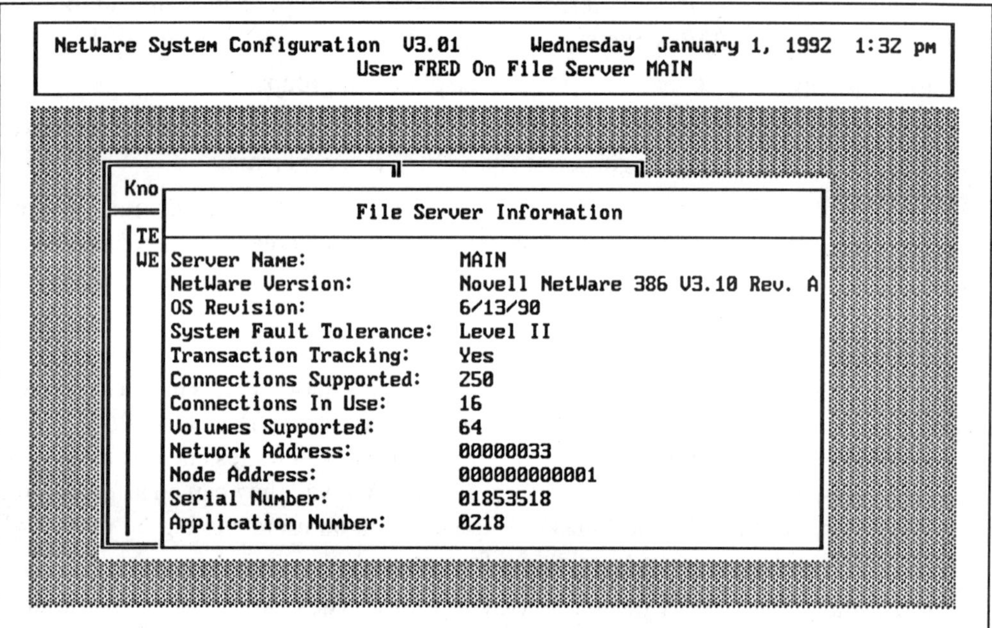

4. To exit SYSCON, press **Alt-F10**, then press **Enter**.
5. Turn to Module 51 to continue the learning sequence.

Module 87
SYSTIME
(ver 2.x and 3.x)

DESCRIPTION

The public command SYSTIME displays the current time and date of the fileserver and sets your workstation accordingly. You can include a fileserver name or view the time of the default server by omitting the name. The syntax is:

```
SYSTIME File_server_name
```

APPLICATIONS

Like DOS, *NetWare* keeps track of the date and time of the last update to each file. It is important for each workstation's internal clock to match the fileserver's. Otherwise, this date/time stamping scheme can become erroneous and, therefore, of no use.

TYPICAL OPERATION

In this activity you check the time and date of the default fileserver. Begin at the DOS prompt of a logged-in workstation.

1. Type **SYSTIME** and press **Enter**. Your display shows a time and date such as:

```
F:\INN>SYSTIME
Current System Time:    Wednesday  January  1,  1992  6:23 pm

F:\INN>
```

2. Turn to Module 91 to continue the learning sequence.

Module 88
TIME
(ver 2.x and 3.x)

DESCRIPTION

The console command TIME displays the fileserver's current date and time. This is maintained by the fileserver as long as it is running. Today, most fileservers also maintain the current date and time while turned off. Under *NetWare* 3.x, this can also be used from a workstation via RCONSOLE (Module 72).

APPLICATIONS

Use TIME to verify that the correct date and time are set on the fileserver. If incorrect, they can be changed with SET TIME (see Module 82).

TYPICAL OPERATION

In this activity you display the current date and time according to the fileserver's internal clock. Begin at the : prompt of your fileserver.

1. Type **TIME** and press **Enter**. You see a display similar to the following:

```
:TIME
Wednesday  January 1, 1992  6:24:25 pm
:
```

2. Turn to Module 82 to continue the learning sequence.

Module 89
TLIST
(ver 2.x and 3.x)

DESCRIPTION

TLIST is a public command that lists the current trustees of given directories and their rights. Trustee rights are assigned using GRANT (see Module 41) or SYSCON (see Module 86). The rights include

READ	Open file and read contents.
WRITE	Open file and write to it.
CREATE	Create new files and directories.
ERASE	Delete files and directories.
MODIFY	Change file or directory name or attributes.
FILE SCAN	See files (but not necessarily open them).
ACCESS CONTROL	Grant file or directory rights to other users.
SUPERVISORY	Under 3.x, this grants all rights and overrides any other restrictions that have been placed on this user within this directory structure.

Trustees are users or groups who have been granted any rights in a given directory. Follow the TLIST command by a directory name, then optionally, a keyword. The keyword "USERS" lists only users; "GROUPS" lists only groups. If neither is used, all trustees are listed.

APPLICATIONS

It is vital to network security to keep track of which users (or groups) have various rights within different directories. TLIST gives quick access to this information. Used in conjunction with GRANT, REMOVE, and REVOKE (see modules 41, 73, and 75), TLIST provides command line management of trustee rights.

TYPICAL OPERATION

In this activity you list all trustees of directory SYS:INN (created in Module 8). Begin at the DOS prompt of a logged-in workstation.

1. Type **TLIST SYS:INN**. Your display shows something like this:

```
F:\INN>TLIST SYS:INN

MAIN\SYS:INN
User trustees:
  JAMES                                    [ R    F ] JAMES FOITEK
  MIKUS                                    [ R  EMF ] MIKE MIKUS
No group trustees.

F:\INN>
```

2. Turn to Module 75 to continue the learning sequence.

Module 90
USERLIST
(ver 2.x and 3.x)

DESCRIPTION

USERLIST is a public command used to list the current users on given fileservers. The list of users includes their connection number and their log-in time. Use this command alone for a list of users on the current default fileserver. Or, you can specify fileservers following the command, as well as specific usernames. The *NetWare* convention of

    FILESERVER NAME/USERNAME

applies and the DOS wild cards of "*" and "?" can be used. The USERLIST command can be followed by any of the three following flags.

A (Address)	This flag will include the physical network address of the workstation for each user.
C (Continuous)	This flag causes the information reported by USERRLIST to scroll continuously on your screen. Otherwise, you must press a key to continue after every screenfull.
O (Object)	This flag will include the object type of this network connection.

APPLICATIONS

Use USERLIST to determine which users are currently logged in to the network or to specific fileservers. This command is commonly used prior to SEND (see Module 79) to determine what users are available to receive messages.

TYPICAL OPERATION

In this activity you display a list of all users on the network. Then you list only users whose usernames start with F. Begin at the DOS prompt of a logged-in workstation.

1. Type **USERLIST** and press **Enter**. The screen resembles this:

```
F:\INN>USERLIST

User Information for Server MAIN
Connection  User Name         Login Time
----------  ---------------   --------------------
         1  JAMES             1-01-1992  1:02 pm
         4  CHEY_ARCHSVR      1-01-1992  6:08 pm
         6  * FRED            1-01-1992  4:31 pm
         9  TIM               1-01-1992 11:24 am
        14  ETC               1-01-1992  5:40 pm
        17  MIKUS             1-01-1992  5:55 pm

F:\INN>
```

Note the "*" on the screen. This signifies who you are logged in as.

2. Type **USERLIST */T*** and press **Enter**. The screen resembles this:

```
F:\INN>USERLIST */T*

User Information for Server MAIN
Connection  User Name         Login Time
----------  ---------------   --------------------
         9  TIM               1-01-1992 11:24 am

User Information for Server ACCTG
Connection  User Name         Login Time
----------  ---------------   --------------------
         6  TIM               1-01-1992 11:16 am

F:\INN>
```

3. Turn to Module 42 to continue the learning sequence.

Module 91
VOLINFO
(ver 2.x and 3.x)

DESCRIPTION

VOLINFO is a public command used to determine the amount of disk space and the number of directory entries used and available on each volume of the current fileserver. This command is vaguely similar to the DOS CHKDSK command, but they are not interchangeable. VOLINFO should always be used on network drives and CHKDSK on local DOS drives.

APPLICATIONS

The VOLINFO command is useful to monitor the available space on network drives. Periodic use of this command helps to determine in advance the need for additional hard drives or the need for housekeeping (removing unneeded files) on existing drives. Use VOLINFO, along with CHKVOL, in place of the less functional CHKDSK found in DOS.

TYPICAL OPERATION

In this activity you determine the remaining space on the current default drive volume. Begin at the DOS prompt of a logged-in workstation.

1. Type **VOLINFO** and press **Enter**. The screen displays the following:

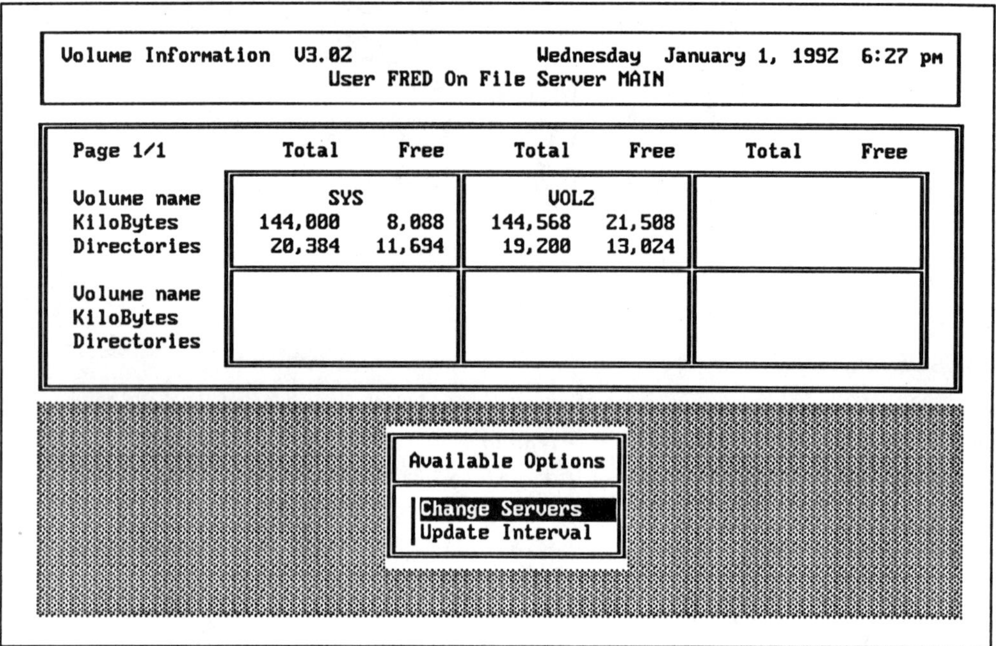

This display is periodically refreshed with updated data until interrupted by the user.

2. If you are on a multiserver network, press **Enter** to select a different fileserver to monitor.

3. If you wish to change the frequency with which this screen is updated, select **Update Interval** and press **Enter**.

4. Press **Esc** to exit this utility and return to a DOS prompt.

5. Turn to Module 17 to continue the learning sequence.

Module 92
WHOAMI
(ver 2.x and 3.x)

DESCRIPTION

WHOAMI is a public command which displays information about the username under which you are logged in. Your connection number (a number that the fileserver temporarily assigns each user at the time of login) and the fileservers to which you are attached are displayed. You may follow the command with a fileserver name, certain flag, or both. The following flags provide additional information about your current status. The full names or abbreviations can be used. If you wish to use any of these flags, follow the command WHOAMI with a forward slash and then the flag.

A (All)	This flag displays all information available with WHOAMI.
C (Continuous)	This flag causes the information reported by WHOAMI to scroll continuously on your screen. Otherwise, you must press a key to continue after every screenfull.
G (Group)	This flag lists the GROUPS to which your username currently belongs.
O (Object)	This flag includes object supervisor information and lists users and groups being supervised.
R (Rights)	This flag displays all of your rights in all directories. This is similar to the information provided by the RIGHTS command (see Module 76).
S (Security)	This flag lists any security equivalences assigned to your username by SYSCON (see Module 86).
SY (System)	This flag includes general system information.
W (Workgroup)	This flag includes workgroup management information as assigned by SYSCON (Module 86).

APPLICATIONS

Use WHOAMI to determine the username under which you are logged in as well as your log in time. Also, certain privileges of that username can be displayed. An administrator, for instance, can determine who is logged in to an unattended workstation or a user that has more than one username can easily determine how they logged in.

TYPICAL OPERATION

In this activity you determine how you are logged in and to what groups you belong. Begin at the DOS prompt of a logged-in workstation.

1. Type **WHOAMI /G** and press **Enter**. A screen similar to this is displayed:

```
F:\INN>WHOAMI /G
You are user FRED attached to server MAIN, connection 6.
Server MAIN is running NetWare 386 V3.10 Rev. A.
Login time: Wednesday  January  1, 1992  4:31 PM
You are a member of the following groups:
    EVERYONE
    ACCTG


F:\INN>
```

2. Turn to Module 90 to continue the learning sequence.

INTRODUCTION

The following list defines terms related to Novell *NetWare* and networks in general. It is assumed that you have a basic understanding of personal computers and DOS, therefore basic DOS concepts and terminology are not included. For a comprehensive education in DOS, or for a quick reference guide, see Wordware Publishing's *Illustrated MS/PC-DOS*.

Term	*Definition*
Administrator	An individual who's job it is to manage the network. This usually includes defining users, groups, print queues, and network security. Administrators are normally given the security equivalence of SUPERVISOR.
ARCNET	A popular type of network for use with Novell *NetWare*. ARCNET uses a token passing scheme and currently transmits data at up to 2.5 megabytes/second.
CSMA/CD	Carrier Sense Multiple Access Collision Detection. This is the networking scheme used by Ethernet networks. The NIC detects data collisions on the network and retransmits the data.
Console	The screen and keyboard of a fileserver. On nondedicated fileservers there is a *NetWare* command called CONSOLE that transfers the system from the workstation mode to the fileserver console mode.
Console Command	Any of a number of *NetWare* commands that are issued from the fileserver console or a nondedicated fileserver in the console mode.
Console Prompt	The colon that appears at the left edge of the fileserver's screen and indicates that the system is ready for a command to be entered.

Term	Definition
Dedicated Fileserver	A computer whose only purpose is to be a fileserver. It cannot function as a workstation.
Ethernet	A popular type of network for use with Novell *NetWare*. Ethernet uses a CSMA/CD and currently transmits data at up to 10 megabytes/second.
Fileserver	The computer which is the heart of the network. The fileserver contains one or more fixed disks that are shared with the workstations on the network. The fileserver also holds and directs queued print jobs.
Fileserver Name	A unique name assigned to each fileserver on a network at the time of installation.
Group	A definition of user rights and privileges. Groups are defined, then users are assigned to these groups. One user can be assigned to multiple groups.
Log In	The process of using the Login command at a workstation to gain access to the network's resources. This access is limited according to the rights given the username that you use. These rights are established by the network administrator.
Log Out	The process of using the Logout command to end a session on a network, and thereby your ability to access the network's resources. To maintain network security, always log out when leaving your workstation.
Multiserver Network	A network with more than one fileserver. Any user on the network may access any fileserver to which they have been assigned a username.
NetWare	A network operating system by Novell, Inc. This is the software portion of a Novell network, and resides in part on both the fileserver and each workstation.
Network Interface Card	An integrated circuit board that is installed in each fileserver and workstation on a network. It is through this device that the computers communicate, along a cabling system.
NIC	Abbreviation for Network Interface Card.
Node	A workstation, fileserver, communication server, or print server; in other words any computer that is attached to the network.

Term	Definition
Nondedicated Fileserver	A computer that has the combined function of both fileserver and workstation. Two commands (CONSOLE and DOS) are used to toggle the system between these modes. This concept is not supported by all versions of *NetWare*.
Public Command	Any of a group of *NetWare* commands that are issued from network workstations. At the time of installation, *NetWare* places the commands in a directory called SYS:PUBLIC.
Queue	A temporary holding area for print jobs (groups of data that have been sent to network printers). The jobs are accumulated in queues and sent to the appropriate printer as it is ready.
Rights	Privileges assigned to users that allow or deny various types of access to network files or directories. Among these are the ability to Read, Write, Delete, and Modify files.
SFT	This stands for System Fault Tolerant. This version of *NetWare* has the ability to continue functioning in spite of certain failures in network hardware.
Supervisor	A special username that is automatically created at the time of *NetWare* installation. SUPERVISOR has all rights to all files and directories, as well as the ability to access all utilities and to change passwords, login scripts, users, groups, etc. Any user may be assigned supervisor equivalency by the SUPERVISOR.
System Command	A special group of commands that are issued at network workstations. These commands are located in the SYS:SYSTEM directory.
Token Passing	A scheme of network data passing that has each NIC transmitting one at a time. A software "token" is passed from one node to the next, with each NIC only allowed to transmit when it has the token. This concept prevents data collisions.
Username	A unique name assigned to each user on the network. Each username is created and defined in terms of privileges and password by the network administrator.
Volume	A division of hard drive storage. A volume often consists of the entire drive. Directories are created within the volume, and files stored within the directories.

Term	Definition
Wild card	A DOS concept that applies to many *NetWare* commands. There are two wild cards, the * and ? characters. When specifying file or directory names, the * can represent any group of missing characters, and the ? any single character.
Workstation	The individual computers attached to the network from which users run their applications. They can access shared network resources, such as drives and printers.
Workstation Prompt	The standard DOS prompt on the workstation screen which indicates that the computer is ready for its next command. Examples of workstation prompts include "F>" and "C>."

Appendix B
NOVELL COMMANDS AND SYNTAX

Command	Syntax
ATOTAL	ATOTAL
ATTACH	ATTACH *fileserver/username*
BINDFIX	BINDFIX
BINDREST	BINDREST
BROADCAST	BROADCAST *message*
CAPTURE	CAPTURE *option*
CASTOFF	CASTOFF *flags*
CASTON	CASTON
CHKVOL	CHKVOL *fileserver/volume drive*:
CLEAR MESSAGE	CLEAR MESSAGE
CLEAR STATION	CLEAR STATION *station number*
COLORPAL	COLORPAL
COMCHECK	COMCHECK
CONFIG	LOAD CONFIG
CONSOLE	CONSOLE
DCONFIG	DCONFIG
DISABLE LOGIN	DISABLE LOGIN
DISABLE TRANSACTIONS	DISABLE TRANSACTIONS
DISABLE TTS	DISABLE TTS
DISK	DISK
DISMOUNT	DISMOUNT [PACK] *volume number*
DISPLAY NETWORKS	DISPLAY NETWORKS
DISPLAY SERVERS	DISPLAY FILESERVERS
DOS	DOS

Command	Syntax
DOWN	DOWN
ENABLE LOGIN	ENABLE LOGIN
ENABLE TRANSACTIONS	ENABLE TRANSACTIONS
ENABLE TTS	ENABLE TTS
ENDCAP	ENDCAP *option*
FCONSOLE	FCONSOLE
FILER	FILER
FLAG	FLAG *directory/filename flags*
FLAGDIR	FLAGDIR *flag*
GRANT	GRANT *option* FOR *path* TO *username*
HELP	HELP
HIDEFILE	HIDEFILE *directory/filename*
HOLDOFF	HOLDOFF
HOLDON	HOLDON
INSTALL	LOAD INSTALL
LISTDIR	LISTDIR *directory drive: flags*
LOGIN	LOGIN *flags fileserver/username*
LOGOUT	LOGOUT *fileserver*
MAKEUSER	MAKEUSER
MAP	MAP *drive:=directory* (see MAP, for more syntaxes)
MENU	MENU *filename*
MONITOR (2.X)	MONITOR *station number*
MONITOR (3.X)	LOAD MONITOR
MOUNT	MOUNT [PACK] *volume number*
NAME	NAME
NCOPY	NCOPY *source file target file flags*
NDIR	NDIR *path option flag*
NPRINT	NPRINT *directory/filename printer number flags*
NSNIPES	NSNIPES

Command	*Syntax*
OFF	OFF
PAUDIT	PAUDIT
PCONSOLE	PCONSOLE
PRINTCON	PRINTCON
PRINTDEF	PRINTDEF
PSC	PSC PS=*printserver name* P=*printer number flags*
PSTAT	PSTAT *option*
PURGE	PURGE *directory/filename*
REMOVE	REMOVE *user* FROM *path*
RENDIR	RENDIR *path* TO *directory*
REVOKE	REVOKE *option* FOR *path* FROM *username*
RIGHTS	RIGHTS *fileserver/drive:directory*
SALVAGE	SALVAGE
SECURITY	SECURITY
SEND	SEND *message* TO *fileserver/username*
SESSION	SESSION
SET TIME	SET TIME *month/day/year hour:minute:second*
SETPASS	SETPASS *fileserver*
SHOWFILE	SHOWFILE *directory/filename*
SLIST	SLIST *flag*
SMODE	SMODE *path option*
SYSCON	SYSCON
SYSTIME	SYSTIME *fileserver*
TIME	TIME
TLIST	TLIST *path*
USERLIST	USERLIST *fileserver/username*
VOLINFO	VOLINFO
WHOAMI	WHOAMI *fileserver/flags*

Appendix C
NOVELL NETWARE EXERCISES

1. About This Book
    a. Describe the purpose of *NetWare*.
    b. How is the Recommended Learning Sequence used?

2. An Overview of a Novell Network
    a. How many versions of Novell exist today?
    b. Can you upgrade from one version to another?
    c. Does each computer on the network need a network interface card?
    d. Under what circumstance can a fileserver become a workstation?
    e. What is a working copy?
    f. Describe the different versions of *NetWare*.
    g. What is the Hot Fix concept?
    h. Do you need to have a hard drive in the fileserver?
    i. What is a UPS?

3. Hardware Installaton
    a. Why is the cable so important in Ethernet networks?
    b. Can NICs have the same address setting?

4. COMPSURF & ZTEST
    a. What does the ZTEST utility do?
    b. What does the COMPSURF utility do?
    c. Which track on fileserver drives is the most critical?

5. NET$OS
    a. What is NET$OS?
    b. Where is NET$OS located on dedicated fileservers?
    c. How is NET$OS created?

6. SERVER
    a. What programs are loaded in SERVER?
    b. Is SERVER available in *NetWare* 2.X?

7. Workstation Shells
    a. What two programs are included in the shell?
    b. How is IPX generated?

8. Booting the System
   a. What is involved in booting the system?
   b. What is involved in booting the fileserver?
   c. What is a diskless workstation?
   d. Explain bringing a workstation and fileserver down.

9. ATOTAL
   a. What makes ATOTAL valid on a network?
   b. Can you obtain a hard copy?

10. ATTACH
    a. Is ATTACH used before or after LOGIN?
    b. Would you use this command with only one fileserver?

11. BINDFIX
    a. What is a bindery?
    b. What does BINDFIX do first?
    c. Can you run this utility at any time without affecting users?

12. BINDREST
    a. What is BINDREST used for?
    b. List the two files that must be present.

13. BROADCAST
    a. How do you BROADCAST a message to a specific user?
    b. How is the screen cleared?

14. CAPTURE
    a. How many flags exist that affect the way output is printed?
    b. Which flag makes any number of copies?
    c. Which flag restores automatic form feeds?
    d. What is NB?
    e. Which flag would you use to cause immediate printing while in an application?

15. CASTOFF
    a. What is CASTOFF?
    b. Which flag would cause messages from only workstations to be disabled?

16. CASTON
    a. What command does CASTON negate?
    b. Are there any flags available?

17. CHKVOL
    a. Which DOS command does CHKVOL replace?
    b. Explain what can be found using CHKVOL.

18. CLEAR MESSAGE
    a. Can Ctrl-Enter be used to clear messages from a console?

19. CLEAR STATION
    a. Why would you most commonly use CLEAR STATION?
    b. What follows the command?

20. COLORPAL
    a. What does this utility change?
    b. Where is the information for colors stored?

21. COMCHECK
    a. Why would you use COMCHECK?
    b. When is COMCHECK run?
    c. Where is COMCHECK located?

22. CONFIG
    a. Which information is provided by CONFIG?
    b. Will CONFIG list the type?
    c. When is CONFIG useful?

23. CONSOLE
    a. What is a nondedicated fileserver?
    b. Can workstation commands be used from a console?

24. DCONFIG
    a. What can a node include?
    b. What information is stored at the time of configuration?

25. DISABLE LOGIN
    a. What does this command do?
    b. Does it affect workstations already logged in?
    c. When would this command be useful?

26. DISABLE TRANSACTIONS
    a. What is a transaction?
    b. When is TTS resumed?

27. DISK
    a. What information is displayed after the drive number?
    b. What is the *NetWare* 3.X equivalent to DISK?
    c. Which command will discontinue the display?

28. DISMOUNT
    a. What is DISMOUNT informing *NetWare*?
    b. Which command should be used for diskettes?

29. DISPLAY NETWORKS
    a. What does DISPLAY NETWORKS list?
    b. What is displayed for each network?

30. DISPLAY SERVERS
    a. What does DISPLAY SERVERS list?
    b. Is this useful on a network with only one fileserver?
    c. How could you get this same information at a workstation?

31. DOS
    a. Why would you use the command DOS?
    b. Would this command be used on a dedicated fileserver?

32. DOWN
    a. Should workstations be logged in when using DOWN?
    b. Explain what DOWN is actually doing.
    c. Should a network ever be shut off without issuing DOWN?

33. EDIT
    a. What does EDIT most frequently edit?
    b. Can it only EDIT files located on the fileserver?

34. ENABLE LOGIN
    a. What does ENABLE LOGIN negate?
    b. Is this command issued from a workstation?

35. ENABLE TRANSACTIONS
    a. Is this command issued from a workstation?
    b. What is the command when using *NetWare* 2.X?

36. ENDCAP
    a. What does ENDCAP do?
    b. Besides manually, when is ENDCAP issued?
    c. What is the difference between the Cancel and CALL flag?

37. FCONSOLE
    a. Is FCONSOLE most useful on 2.X or 3.X servers?
    b. Do you need supervisor privileges to BROADCAST?
    c. Can you DOWN the fileserver through FCONSOLE?
    d. What does the menu selection Statistics tell you?

38. FILER
    a. What are trustees?
    b. What information is displayed regarding a directory?
    c. What information can be changed from within FILER?

39. FLAG
    a. What will happen if a path or filename is not specified?
    b. Which flag would be used to prevent users from modifying specific files?
    c. When is the S flag used?

40. FLAGDIR
    a. What is the difference between FLAGDIR and FLAG?
    b. What does the N flag cancel?
    c. What is the only flag that is available in 2.X only?

41. GRANT
    a. In which menu utility is GRANT also found?
    b. What is the difference with GRANT in 2.X and 3.X?
    c. Give an example of the syntax of GRANT.

42. HELP
    a. Can you access help from any directory?
    b. How do you exit HELP?
    c. What is the simpler way of using HELP?

43. HIDEFILE
    a. Does HIDEFILE protect a file from deletion?
    b. Can wildcards be used?

44. HOLDOFF
    a. What command is negated by HOLDOFF?
    b. What does HOLDOFF reinstate?

45. HOLDON
    a. What does HOLDON lock?
    b. Can the file be printed when HOLDON has been used?

46. INSTALL
    a. When is INSTALL used?
    b. Is it available in *NetWare* 2.X?
    c. What does PARTITION TABLES allow you to create?
    d. If a partition is deleted, can it be salvaged?
    e. How do you create new volumes?

47. LISTDIR
    a. Which DOS command is similar to LISTDIR?
    b. Which flag would be used to have the creation date and time displayed?

48. LOGIN
    a. Will there always be a password for every user?
    b. Under what circumstance(s) would you not specify a server?
    c. What does the flag C cause?

49. LOGOUT
    a. When is it not necessary to specify a server?
    b. Should you LOGOUT even if only leaving your workstation for a few minutes?

50. LOGIN SCRIPTS
    a. Can LOGIN SCRIPTS be assigned with MAKEUSER?
    b. Who can change the SYSTEM LOGIN SCRIPT?
    c. Why would you use the command EXIT in a LOGIN SCRIPT?

51. MAKEUSER
    a. Which menu utility could also be used in place of MAKEUSER?
    b. Which extension must be given to the test file?
    c. How should each instruction line start?
    d. What instruction line limits the number of workstations a user may be logged into at once?

52. MAP
    a. Which DOS command is similar to MAP?
    b. Can drive names be any letter?
    c. What will the flag INS do for you?

53. MENU
    a. What is the syntax for MENU?
    b. What extension must the text file have?
    c. What must precede the first line?

54. MONITOR (vers 3.X)
    a. What happens if MONITOR is left on the screen for too long?
    b. Which information will be displayed?
    c. Which selection will let you select a file and report on the current use of that file?

55. MONITOR (vers 2.X)
    a. Can MONITOR be displayed from the workstation?
    b. What is displayed across the top of the screen?
    c. How is the information forced to update?

56. MOUNT
    a. What does MOUNT inform *NetWare*?
    b. Under which version can *NetWare* span more than one drive?
    c. Under 3.X must *NetWare* be told to MOUNT nonremovable volumes?

57. NAME
    a. When are fileservers named under 2.X?

58. NCOPY
    a. What DOS command is similar to NCOPY?
    b. Give an example of the syntax of NCOPY.

59. NDIR
    a. What does NDIR list?
    b. Can wildcards be used?
    c. What parameter would list all files created on the parameter date?
    d. What does the BRIEF flag do?

60. NPRINT
    a. Which DOS command is similar to NPRINT?
    b. What is the syntax for NPRINT?
    c. Why is this faster than the DOS command?
    d. What flag would you use to suppress a banner page?

61. NSNIPES
    a. Play a game of NSNIPES.

62. OFF
    a. Which DOS command is similar to OFF?
    b. Under 2.X which command does this negate?
    c. Can this command be issued from a workstation?

63. PAUDIT
    a. Under what circumstances is PAUDIT valid?
    b. How do you receive a hard copy of this report?
    c. Should this file always be there?

64. PCONSOLE
    a. What does PCONSOLE allow you to do?
    b. What is a print queue?
    c. What will the selection Queue Servers tell you?

65. PRINTCON
    a. What does PRINTCON allow to be created?
    b. What is an alternate way of exiting PRINTCON?
    c. What flag would you use to specify someone else's username on the banner page?
    d. What will the flag Enable Timeout cause?

66. PRINTDEF
    a. What are print devices?
    b. Do the codes vary from printer to printer?
    c. Where do you find the printer code information?
    d. What is a print mode?

67. PRINTER
    a. What is a queue?
    b. Is there always a queue for each printer?
    c. Can these commands be issued from a workstation?

68. PSC
    a. What does PSC tell you?
    b. What does the flag CD do?
    c. What is the syntax for PSC?

70. PSTAT
    a. If the P= flag is omitted, what will PSTAT report?
    b. Can this be executed from a workstation?

71. PURGE
    a. What is the difference between 2.X and 3.X in terms of managing deleted files?
    b. When do erased files get PURGEd under 3.X?
    c. Can wildcards be used?

73. REMOVE
    a. What is REMOVEd when this command is issued?
    b. Where else can this same action be accomplished?

74. **RENDIR**
    a.   What does this command do to directories?
    b.   What is the syntax?
    c.   Are the rights maintained for the new directory?

75. **REVOKE**
    a.   What does this command remove?
    b.   What is the difference between REVOKE and REMOVE?
    c.   What is the syntax?

76. **RIGHTS**
    a.   What menu-driven utility can give you the same information?
    b.   Which right allows you to list files in a directory?
    c.   Which right is only valid under 3.X?

77. **SALVAGE**
    a.   Can you SALVAGE files that have been PURGEd?
    b.   Can you SALVAGE a directory under 2.X?

78. **SECURITY**
    a.   What does SECURITY do?
    b.   How do you obtain a hard copy of this report?

79. **SEND**
    a.   Where is the message displayed?
    b.   How is a message cleared from the workstation?
    c.   How do you send a message to a fileserver?
    d.   What menu-driven utility also allows the sending of messages?

80. **SESSION**
    a.   Which menu selection allows you to determine your default drive?
    b.   List the *NetWare* command being accomplished through each menu selection.

81. **SETPASS**
    a.   What menu-drive utility will also let you assign a password?
    b.   If you already have a password will SETPASS allow you to change it?

82. **SET TIME**
    a.   Will this command change a workstation's time?
    b.   What would be the correct entry for 3:00 p.m.?

83. **SHOWFILE**
    a.   What command does SHOWFILE reverse?
    b.   Can you use wildcards in naming a file to show?

84. SLIST
    a. What will SLIST list?
    b. Would you use this command on a single-server network?

85. SMODE
    a. What does SMODE determine?
    b. Explain where *NetWare* will search if mode 1 is used.

86. SYSCON
    a. What options are available under Supervisor Options?
    b. What does "accounting" track?
    c. How would you disable someone's account?

87. SYSTIME
    a. Does this command "only" display the current time and date?
    b. What is the syntax?

88. TIME
    a. Under what condition can this command be issued from a workstation?

89. TLIST
    a. What is a trustee?
    b. If neither USER or GROUP is used, what is listed?
    c. How are trustee rights assigned?

90. USERLIST
    a. When is this command commonly used?
    b. What is listed on the screen beside the list of users?

91. VOLINFO
    a. What DOS command is similar to VOLINFO?
    b. Can VOLINFO be used on local drives?

92. WHOAMI
    a. What flag will display any security equivalences assigned to your username?

Index

Other Books from Wordware Publishing, Inc.

Computer Aided Drafting
Illustrated AutoCAD (Release 10)
Illustrated AutoCAD (Release 11)
Illustrated AutoLISP
Illustrated AutoSketch 2.0
Illustrated Generic CADD Level 3

Database Management
Illustrated dBASE III Plus
Illustrated dBASE IV 1.1
Illustrated Force 2
Illustrated FoxPro
Illustrated FoxPro 2.0
Illustrated Paradox 3.0 Volume II (2nd Ed.)

Desktop Publishing
The Desktop Studio: Multimedia with the Amiga
Illustrated PFS:First Publisher 2.0 & 3.0
Illustrated PageMaker 4.0
Illustrated Ventura 3.0 (Windows Ed.)
Illustrated Ventura 3.0 (DOS/GEM Ed.)
Illustrated Ventura 4.0

General and Advanced Topics
111 Clipper Functions
The Complete Communications Handbook
Financial Modeling using Lotus 1-2-3
GUI Programming with C
Illustrated DacEasy Accounting 4.1
Illustrated DacEasy Accounting 4.2
Illustrated Harvard Graphics 2.3
Illustrated Harvard Graphics 3.0
Illustrated Novell NetWare 2.x/3.x
Novell NetWare: Adv. Tech. and Applications
Understanding 3COM Networks
Using Your Modem

Integrated
Illustrated Enable/OA
Illustrated Framework III
Illustrated Microsoft Works 2.0
Illustrated Q&A 3.0 (2nd Ed.)
Illustrated Q&A 4.0

Programming Languages
Illustrated C Programming (ANSI) (2nd Ed.)
Illustrated Clipper 5.0 (2nd Ed.)
Illustrated QBasic for MS-DOS 5.0
Graphics Programming with Turbo Pascal
Illustrated Turbo C++
Illustrated Turbo Debugger 3.0
Illustrated Turbo Pascal 6.0

Spreadsheet
Illustrated Excel 4.0 for Windows
Illustrated Lotus 1-2-3 Rel. 2.2
Illustrated Lotus 1-2-3 Rel. 3.0
Illustrated Quattro
Illustrated SuperCalc 5

Systems and Operating Guides
Illustrated DR DOS 6.0
Illustrated MS-DOS 5.0
Illustrated UNIX System V
Illustrated Windows 3.0
Illustrated Windows 3.1

Word Processing
Illustrated Microsoft Word 5.0 (PC)
Illustrated Word for Windows
Illustrated WordPerfect 1.0 (Macintosh)
Illustrated WordPerfect 5.1
Illustrated WordPerfect for Windows
Illustrated WordStar 6.0
WordPerfect Wizardry Adv. Tech. and Applications

Popular Applications Series
Build Your Own Computer
Cost Control Using Lotus 1-2-3
Creating Newsletters with Ventura
Desktop Publishing with Word 2.0 for Windows
Desktop Publishing with WordPerfect
Learn AutoCAD in a Day
Learn CorelDRAW! in a Day
Learn dBASE in a Day
Learn DOS in a Day
Learn DrawPerfect in a Day
Learn Excel for Windows in a Day
Learn FoxPro 2.0 in a Day
Learn Harvard Graphics 3.0 in a Day
Learn Lotus 1-2-3 in a Day
Learn Microsoft Works in a Day
Learn Pacioli 2000 in a Day
Learn PageMaker 4.0 in a Day
Learn PAL in a Day
Learn Paradox in a Day
Learn Paradox for Windows in a Day
Learn PC Paintbrush in a Day
Learn PlanPerfect in a Day
Learn Quattro Pro in a Day
Learn Quicken in a Day
Learn Ventura 4.0 in a Day
Learn Windows in a Day
Learn Word 2.0 for Windows in a Day
Learn WordPerfect for Windows in a Day
Learn WordPerfect in a Day (2nd Ed.)
Mailing Lists using dBASE
Object-Oriented Programming using Turbo C++
Presentations with Harvard Graphics
WordPerfect Macros
Write Your Own Programming Language using C++

Regional
Classic Clint: The Laughs and Times of Clint
   Murchison, Jr.
Exploring the Alamo Legends
Forget the Alamo
The Great Texas Airship Mystery
100 Days in Texas: The Alamo Letters
Rainy Days in Texas Funbook
San Antonio Uncovered
Texas Highway Humor
Texas Tales Your Teacher Never Told You
Texas Wit and Wisdom
That Cat Won't Flush
They Don't Have to Die
This Dog'll Hunt
To the Tyrants Never Yield
Unsolved Texas Mysteries

Call Wordware Publishing, Inc. for names of the bookstores in your area
(214) 423-0090